OPERATIONALLY SPEAKING

An Event Operations Guide

3RD Edition

By Frank K. Bussey

"If you want to know how to run a major golf event, you should go to someone who has run them for years--successfully. That's Frank Bussey, This book is the how-to from someone that knows EXACTLY how-to."

John Feinstein, American Sportswriter and Commentator

Printed by
Sports Operations LLC
frankbussey@sportsoperations.com

ISBN: 978-0-578-15807-5
3rd Edition

COVER DESIGN BY GROUP W ART WORKS AND GROUNDLINKX LLC

Preface

This book contains information about what it takes to operate a major golf event. This information may be applied to any event, as all events contain the same elements. However, you may need to reduce the number of people in different areas for a small event such as security and parking personnel.

It will be based upon my experience over the last 40 years of operating events such as United States Open Golf Championships, International Players Tennis Championships, World Cup Polo Championships, and similar large events.

When asked what I do, it is hard to explain to people who are not in the business. So to simplify, I tell them I build a temporary city for 50,000 people, including all the amenities, tear it down after the event, and restore it to its original condition.

Most people see only the venue on television and never understand the ancillary things that occur outside the ropes.

This book will discuss those things.

The main goal of operations is to finish the site setup, run the event efficiently, and remove it on time and within budget. To do this, a great deal of information needs to be assembled. Once well-planned, it is essential to guide your vendors and staff effectively to achieve a successful outcome.

There will be problems along the way. No event can escape this fact, but it is how you deal with them that will make the difference. Situations can change very quickly and you need to be prepared to address them immediately to limit them from spiraling out of control.

This book will assist in planning your event. It is only a guide; experience will be paramount to gain proficiency in the operation of any event.

Also, it is very important to maintain a sense of humor during any event, as the things you are likely to see and deal with will definitely make you laugh.

Dedication

I am dedicating this book to all the operations people who endure the rigorous demands on their life to put on an event, any event. The long hours, the missed lunches and dinners and the torment of knowing the big ball is rolling and the event will start whether you are ready or not.

This book is also dedicated to my wife Jaymie, the love of my life. Her faith and support were the driving factors in completing this book.

I would also like to thank my brother Sam. Without his insight and asking questions, from a layman's point of view, this book could never have evolved.

A special thanks to my editor, Karen Moraghan, of Hunter Public Relations * Special Events. Her talent to find the best format without sacrificing intent or style is truly amazing.

A very special thanks to my other brother Jim for assisting with the editing of the 3rd edition. It is truly appreciated.

Through the Grace of God all things are possible.

Table of Contents

Illustrations

Illustrations

Chapter One

SITE REVIEW

This chapter is a basic review of the event site. Each area will be discussed in depth in later chapters. The overall site is reviewed initially for basic areas: corporate tent locations, media compound, vendor compound space, parking areas close to the site, and a convenient bus shuttle drop off for spectators. Also trees need to be considered when reviewing any site. Will they hinder the location that you want for facilities? Can they be transplanted if necessary? Is the venue willing to remove the trees entirely?

You can squeeze facilities against trees if you still maintain the ability to raise tents without hitting the branches. The topography needs to be considered during this process, as height will be added to the tents if they are located on hills. If you are to maintain a level floor, the added floor height above the ground will cost you additional money. If relatively flat areas can be found, then the rest will follow. I will show some examples in Chapter Three.

The Corporate entertainment tents are usually located near the clubhouse, adjacent to player putting greens, driving range, and active or inactive fairways. The value of the corporate tents is based largely on the location as well as the amenities offered as part of the package, which will be discussed later. Corporate clients will also rely on the event's ability to get them to and from the site with relative ease.

Vendor compound space is paramount if you expect your vendors to perform their tasks on a timely basis. Each area needs to be large enough for tractor trailers to off-load material and turn around, as well as to store equipment. This part is the biggest challenge. There have been times when trucks needed to off-load at another location so they can leave and the material is moved by forklift to the designated locations. Depending upon the distance away from the site, the equipment may need to be reloaded on smaller trucks and then off-loaded again at the needed location.

In addition, the television networks have a tendency to require a lot of space, depending upon the size of the event. Be sure to address this in your space calculations. All the networks that will be televising, including the foreign networks, need adequate space for office trailers, production trucks, dining facilities, and parking. These space requirements have increased, as most televised events are produced in high definition which requires more production trucks.

Depending upon the number of people expected at the event, adequate parking areas need to be provided. Gone are the days when spectators could park adjacent to the site and walk across the street to enter, unless it is a very small event. In most cases, the closest parking to accommodate the numbers of cars could be up to 12 miles away and require shuttle buses to transport spectators to the site. Spectator flow around the site should also be given some thought. If the site is jammed with tents, trucks, and other obstructions, is there still enough room to move the spectators around the site easily?

The spectator drop-off area should be close to the site, if not on the property itself. The spectators will appreciate the closeness to a bus pick-up at the end of the day, having walked around all day. It should have enough space to stage at least eight full size buses.

In this case, more is better, due to the volume of crowds leaving at the end of the day. Ease of entry to and from the event is very important. Traffic patterns around

the venue need to be explored carefully. Will the event cause so much congestion that it will have a negative impact on the event itself?

This point will be discussed in Chapter 15: Parking and Traffic.

In most cases, there should be a retail merchandise pavilion tent, depending upon the type of event. Normally this tent is very large and would rival Macy's, world famous department store, interior...Sometimes there is an area that is sold to individual retail vendors, and you would get a percentage of sales. History shows it is best located somewhere by the main entrance or spectator drop-off.

The media compound location and size will be determined by the size of the event and the types of coverage you expect it to receive. Large events can have upwards of 1200 media people on site covering the event: writers from major newspapers, photographers, local networks, and radio stations, as well as foreign correspondents.

There needs to be space for all the support facilities that go hand in hand with this large operation. These facilities might include an interview tent, dining tent, photographers lounge, and support trailers for scoring, Internet access, and darkrooms.

You will find that these elements hold true for any event. If you are starting an event from the ground up, it will be helpful to review all these items before looking for a potential site.

For instance, it would be real shame if you have a great venue, but no way to get the people to or from the site.

All of these things will be discussed within the chapters of this book.

Chapter Two

MAPPING

There is an old way to map out the facilities on a golf course or any outdoor event. The old way was to call around to aerial photo companies to determine if they had an aerial of your site. If you find one, has it been flown recently enough to accurately depict the current site? If the aerial is suitable, you would have the aerial mapping company enlarge the photo. You would then trace the areas, using onionskin paper. You would depict fairways, greens, tees, and structures, and have these items added to the Mylar,a heavy plastic film, so you could draw in your facilities. Having done so, you would take the Mylar to a blueprint company to make blueprints of the map for you.

If there was no recent aerial available, you would need to have the aerial company fly over and prepare an aerial photo for your use per the specifications mentioned above.

The next step would be to contract an architect to add the features on the map. These would include tents, trailers, and bleachers, but you may need security and hazardous material locations as well.

Each time an architect touched the Mylar, it would be an additional expense and time.

The map might be revised a dozen times or more, and each time it would incur an expense.

However, there is a new way.

There is proprietary GIS (geographic information system) software called Golf Course Analytics, which was specifically designed for golf and other outdoor events. This software allows you to take the plan out of the architect's hands and place it in yours. I have been using this software for a number of years, and it has become invaluable in the planning and execution of events.

This program sits on top of an orthorectified, digitized aerial photograph. Orthorectification is a very accurate process that uses space-age technology to remove up to 99% of aerial photo distortions, so that the measurements anywhere on the photograph are representative of the corresponding areas on the ground. A digital map is then created of the event site in different layers (i.e., tents, trailers, bleachers and so on).

This affords the ability to open all of the layers or only a few, depending on what you are trying to achieve. Each layer has a browser window which, when opened, lists everything on that layer. You may add headings to the browser to custom fit the desired information for display.

This program and similar programs are instrumental in space planning a site. You have the ability to see what fits in a particular location, without actually taking field measurements. However, before finalizing your plans, field measuring should be the norm.

This is necessary due to the topography of the ground and when areas are particularly tight. You might find that the tents are too close to each other to be erected, for example, or there is a transformer in the middle of one tent that doesn't show up on the aerial.

I have looked at the maps I generated in the past by the old method. They are unattractive and could only have been used for in house purposes. There are erasures shown on the map, and the tents in the villages are grouped as one block.

Alternatively, the software is invaluable for placement of portopots, dumpsters, bleachers, office trailers, tents, decks, temporary roads, rope lines, fencing, and much more. I have used it to create a sign plan, complete with directional arrows for spectators, and a separate plan for parking routes and lots. I displayed security posts pre-, during and post- event. I also used it to show the medical coverage areas for the paramedic crews. The resulting maps and diagrams are very professional and may be shared with vendors and corporate supporters.

My advice is to use such a program whenever possible; it will save you a lot of time and money.

All factors considered, it is more cost effective and certainly more presentable to have the program. And you can make changes as you go without any time lost. I have included some pictures to illustrate throughout the book.

Some of the areas in which this program would be beneficial are listed below.

Security: Security stations can be displayed in the necessary locations. An extensive listing of the stations is available, showing the times needed, location of each guard, total hours, rate per hour and cost. Additional columns in the database can be added to display what you need.

Tents: This layer allows you to try different sizes to see what fits best in a specific location. You'll know immediately. There is a full-featured selection of tent styles and colors. The program has the capability of tracking all the tents by size, location, price and name, or designs from your own database, if desired.

Fencing: The fencing layer allows the use of different styles to show the various heights and types of fence. It has a feature that will display the length of each piece. A database can also be created showing summaries of each fence type.

Restroom Facilities: This layer will show the placement of restroom facilities throughout the site, so you can to see immediately if the numbers are correct for your event by using the summation tool, which adds all the units you have on the map. You can review the database for the quantities in each area.

Support trailers: You have the opportunity to see where you have located the trailers on the site. You can distinguish between office trailers and others by changing the color of each type. The program can track by size, location, type, length of rental period, and anything else you may want to add.

Traffic Patterns: You will have the ability to show the bus and car traffic patterns around the site. Shuttle routes can be displayed as well.

Law enforcement will ask for these maps as well as others which might show necessary traffic officer placement.

Parking: If you outline an area, the program will show the number of cars which can fit in the designated location using a formula. We will delve deeper into this formula later, in Chapter 15.

I could go on with more uses for the program, but it already sounds like a sales job. There are many programs on the market similar to this one. This one works for me.

You will need to search out the best option for your needs.

All of the maps and databases illustrated in this book have been made by using the Golf Course Analytics software program.

Get with the program.

These are examples of some of the types of databases you can create within the mapping program.

SECURITY DATA

Number	Location	Date	Time	Hours	Days	People	Total
D28	Golf Shop-Security-Theft	June 12- June 18	7am-10pm	15	7	1	105
D29	Golf Shop-Security-Theft	June 12- June 18	7am-10pm	15	7	1	105
D30	Golf Shop-Security-Theft	June 12- June 18	7am-10pm	15	7	1	105
D31	US Open Store-Security-Theft	June 12- June 18	6am-10pm	16	7	1	112
D32	US Open Store-Security-Theft	June 12- June 18	6am-10pm	16	7	1	112
D33	Iron Gate-Car Passes	June 12- June 18	6am-10pm	16	7	1	112
D34	Putting Green- Crowd Control	June 12- June 18	6am-6pm	12	7	1	84
D35	Putting Green-Crowd Control	June 12- June 18	6am-6pm	12	7	1	84
D36	Post Office Lot- Car Passes	June 12- June 18	6am-7pm	13	7	1	91
D37	Post Office Lot-Car Passes	June 12- June 18	6am-7pm	13	7	1	91
D38	Wells Fargo Lot-Car Passes,Credentials	June 12- June 18	6am-7pm	13	7	1	91
D39	Wells Fargo Lot-Traffic Control	June 12- June 18	6am-7pm	13	7	1	91
D40	Pro Shop Patio-Crowd Control	June 12- June 18	6am-3pm	9	7	1	63

BLEACHER DATA

Name	Location	Size	Row	Capacity
Bleacher	3rd Green	28x63	9	292
Bleacher	3rd Green	28x49	9	220
Bleacher	1st Green	44x70	15	544
Bleacher	4th Tee	49x52	18	436
Bleacher	4th Tee	21x36	12	122
Bleacher	4th Green	70x60	21	760
Bleacher	5th Green	44x84	15	696
Bleacher	6th Green	44x112	15	812
Bleacher	7th Green	60x70	21	760
Bleacher	8th Green	68x112	24	1,350
Bleacher	9th Green	36x42	12	266
Bleacher	10th Green	42x36	12	266
Bleacher	12th Green	49x36	12	292
Bleacher	12th Green	49x36	12	292
Bleacher	12th Green	49x36	12	292
Bleacher	13th Green	52x84	18	834

This is a typical database for the fencing which can be used around the site. There is a tool within the mapping program which will give you the totals of each size fence at a touch of a button.

FENCE DATA

InstallationDate	Four	Fourvinyl	Six	Eight	Location
June 2	0	0	158	0	Pavillion
June 2	0	0	39	0	Pavillion Admissions
June 2	0	0	448	0	Tennis Courts Perimeter
May 29	0	0	0	65	Merchandise Tent
June 1	0	0	301	0	14 Tee to Whitman Lane
June 4	0	0	60	0	3rd Fairway Corporate
June 4	21	0	0	0	3rd Fairway Corporate Deck
June 8	0	0	288	0	Tennis Courts Front Perimeter
May 25	0	0	614	0	Beetle Farm Will Call Perimeter

TRAILER DATA

Name	Number	Location	Size	SqFt	AC
Food & Beverage F&B	11	Triangle	40x40	1,600	
prep F&B	12	Triangle	20x20	400	
Concession F&B	15	12 Green	20x20	400	
Concession F&B	16	Old 5 Green	20x20	400	
Concession F&B	17	Beach Club	30x50	1,500	
Cash Concession F&B	19	Behind Equestrian Center	40x40	1,600	
Media	21	Beetle Farm	100x200	19,404	38,808
Media Dining	22	Beetle Farm	50x100	4,802	9604
Will Call Canopy	23	Beetle Farm	10x40	400	
Shipping	24	Peter Hay	10x10	100	
Concession F&B	25	Peter Hay	10x10	100	

I have created categories within this database, which are the headers on the spreadsheet. you can add or delete these, as your preferences may change. All of the tents are numbered to help the building department keep track. The location and size explains to the tent vendor where the tent is located and the size of the tent.

I added the square footages, as most air conditioning costs are based upon square footage.

TENT DATA

Name	Number	Location	Size	SqFt	AC
Food & Beverage F&B	11	Triangle	40x40	1,600	
prep F&B	12	Triangle	20x20	400	
Concession F&B	15	12 Green	20x20	400	
Concession F&B	16	Old 5 Green	20x20	400	
Concession F&B	17	Beach Club	30x50	1,500	
Cash Concession F&B	19	Behind Equestrian Center	40x40	1,600	
Media	21	Beetle Farm	100x200	19,404	38,808
Media Dining	22	Beetle Farm	50x100	4,802	9604
Will Call Canopy	23	Beetle Farm	10x40	400	
Shipping	24	Peter Hay	10x10	100	
Concession F&B	25	Peter Hay	10x10	100	

Below is an example of a trailer database. Every trailer is numberedwith the type, size, arrival and departure dates, number of months rented, and the number of steps needed. A column for cost per unit may also be added.

Name	Location	Number	Size	Arrive	Depart	Months	Steps
Beverage Refrigerator	Equestrian	44	0	0	0	0	0
Commissary	Behind Equestrian Cente	2	8x32	521	621	1	1
Unisys	Tennis Court Parking Lot	33	12x60	521	621	1	2
Scoring Central	Beetle Farm	34	10x48	521	621	1	2
Media	Beetle Farm	36	8x32	521	621	1	2
US Championship Network	Beetle Farm	35	8x32	521	621	1	2
Will Call	Beetle Farm	37	10x48	521	621	1	2
Medical	Beetle Farm	38	8x32	521	621	1	2
Security	Beetle Farm	39	8x32	521	621	1	2
Container	Peter Hay	49	0	0	0	0	0

Chapter Three

FACILITY PLACEMENT

Facilities are components that need to occupy space at the site. This is very important, because you and everyone else will have to live with the placement of all the facilities. You will need to know the size of the tents you are using and the dimensions of the trailers before you can adequately plan.

Assume that all tents will have some kind of wood flooring, unless the event is perpetual, in which case you can have more permanent asphalt pads laid. The flooring can be of two types: either level flooring or contour, which follows the elevation of the ground. If the slope is too severe, don't skimp - go with level flooring. It may cost a bit more, but it is much better in the long run. You don't want your guests sitting on a tilted floor; it tends to spill drinks.

This is an example of the construction of level flooring. Notice the scaffolding on the left of the picture and the 4"x6" beams on top of the scaffolding. Plywood will be screwed to the beams and carpet installed on top of the plywood, as shown below.

The same holds true for decking. You may be able to use contour flooring for walkways, as you are really only concerned about wet ground. But again, if the ground is too hilly, go with level flooring. Wherever you have flooring, you will want to put a covering on top of the wood. Bare wood is not the image you are trying to achieve. People have paid a lot of money for their experience, and bare wood flooring will cheapen the look. Astroturf or carpet are the norm. Don't forget to add this to the budget.

The placement of the corporate tents is first and foremost, due to the revenue they produce.

Hopefully, you know the size each tent needs to be to maximize potential. The marketing team should have conducted this research. That being said, you need to leave some room between the tents for heating and air conditioning condensers, if air or heat is going to be used. Make sure trees don't come too close to the tents; otherwise, the tent company will have a problem raising the tents. On occasion, I have had to find the personnel to trim branches. Otherwise, the tent could not be raised.

This is an example of building around trees. This flooring system is call "biljax." "Biljax" floors are 4'x4' square metal frames with plywood inserts that interlock, supported by metal columns that can be adjusted to the correct height. This system is installed faster than the scaffolding and beams, but can only be used to six feet above ground. After six feet, it is recommended that the scaffolding system be used.

You will invariably make some barter deals, which will require additional hospitality tents. These deals might be made with a rental car agency to provide cars for the players and VIPs, vans for evacuation or, depending upon the event, trucks for operations. It also might include the scoring provider or the main television network. The location of these tents will depend on the deal you make. The more cost to the deal, the better a location is expected.

The merchandise tent should be placed in an area of prominence, in a well-trafficked location. This is another profit center, so make sure it is in a place to catch the spectator's eye. Take into consideration the amount of space needed for support facilities for the merchandise pavilion or merchandise area, where space is sold to individual retailers.

These might include a finance trailer, credit card transaction trailer, storage trailers, volunteer check in-trailers, cardboard compactor, restroom trailers, loading docks, and dumpsters, in addition to a small tent for staff to take breaks.

You might want to put additional merchandise outlets on the golf course to insure maximum revenues. Make sure the locations chosen allow you to restock during the event without disrupting play.

The Media Tent could require a lot of space, depending upon the size and prestige of your event. It should include space for working media, dining, interview area, and photographers lounge. Another area around the 18th green may be utilized for

quick quotes for the networks.

Surrounding the media tent would be support trailers for scoring, additional photo trailers, or anything else the media director might deem necessary. You must plan for a food prep tent for media dining and the support trailers, which are required by the caterer.

Everything requires space.

Restroom trailers will also need to be provided. The location should be convenient for the media, or as convenient as possible. It would be good if they didn't have to walk 300 yards before reaching the tent, as it tends to make them cranky.

Place your concessions where people can see them. It won't help your revenue if spectators have to search for them. Keep them out of view of your television network coverage and size them to accommodate your anticipated crowds.

Based upon the projected attendance, the concessionaire will be able to determine sizes and how many facilities will be needed on course.

Take into consideration during the location process that these tents will need to be restocked at night with some kind of vehicle, usually a pickup truck. The concessionaire must have room behind each concession for power, waste water, propane tanks, hand washing stations, and storage. These costs are normally borne by the vendor.

Normally, the spectator restroom facilities (portopots) would be placed adjacent to the concession areas and again, they must be the appropriate number for the anticipated crowd.

Check with the building department and your restroom provider if you are unsure about the number of units needed.

Make sure you allow for truck access to all the locations to pump the units. It would be useless to have a great location and not be able to service it.

Enough 30 cubic yard capacity dumpsters should also be strategically placed around the course to ease trash removal. Remember, large trucks need access to these locations, generally at night.

Don't make it too difficult for the drivers; we don't want them running into trees. It is difficult to determine the correct number of dumpsters all of the time. You may find, after the first day, the need to supplement or adjust locations. Bleachers are placed wherever viewing is to be maximized. You will need to consider the existing trees during this process, as sometimes removal of trees will be required prior to bleacher installation.

The biggest concern for facility placement will be necessary vendor compounds. The space for each vendor will be determined by the size of the event. Smaller events will require less space than large events.

Vendors will tell you what want. However, you may negotiate this item. There are few sites that have unlimited compound space, and the available space must be split among all the vendors.

Wherever you choose to place facilities, pay attention to stay away from low-lying areas, due to potential rain, except maybe in parts of California during the summer months. If you are unable to pick high ground for your facilities, you may have to

spread crushed gravel rock in these locations to provide a stabilized surface for your vendors to operate.

If the area is to be used by heavy fork-lifts or trucks, nine inches of compressed rock is the rule. If the area will be used for golf cars or cars, the rule of thumb is 6 inches.

The cost for crushed rock will vary site to site, but a rule of thumb would be around $1.50 per square foot at a depth of six inches. You will use a greater depth than asphalt, to compensate for compaction and losing some into the ground.

If your event is perpetual, and the tents will be the same size and going in the same location every year, you might choose to asphalt the tent pads. The cost for this is approximately $4-$6 per square foot of four-inch asphalt.

If you decide this is the better option, make the pad large enough for the tent footprint and raise the pad at least six inches above ground, to prevent water from entering the tents.

If you think the tent sizes might change, then I would advise against permanent pads until such time the sizes are determined.

Pay particular attention to support vehicle access. You can pick the best location in the world, but if you can't access the location due to lack of roads or cart paths, then it won't work.

At one particular venue, before the mapping program existed, the tents had been installed and the networks came on site to place their cranes. One crane was supposed to slide in between two tents in the village. The space turned out to be two feet too narrow for the crane to fit. Obviously, this was a big problem. The solution was to reduce the tent floor. We had used "biljax" flooring in this case, which extended two feet beyond the tent. We were able to replace the four foot sections of floor on the two tents with two foot sections and the crane could fit.

You need to think of all the possibilities before you throw in the towel; what you come up with may surprise you.

This is an example of the placing facilities placement in tight areas by using a mapping program.

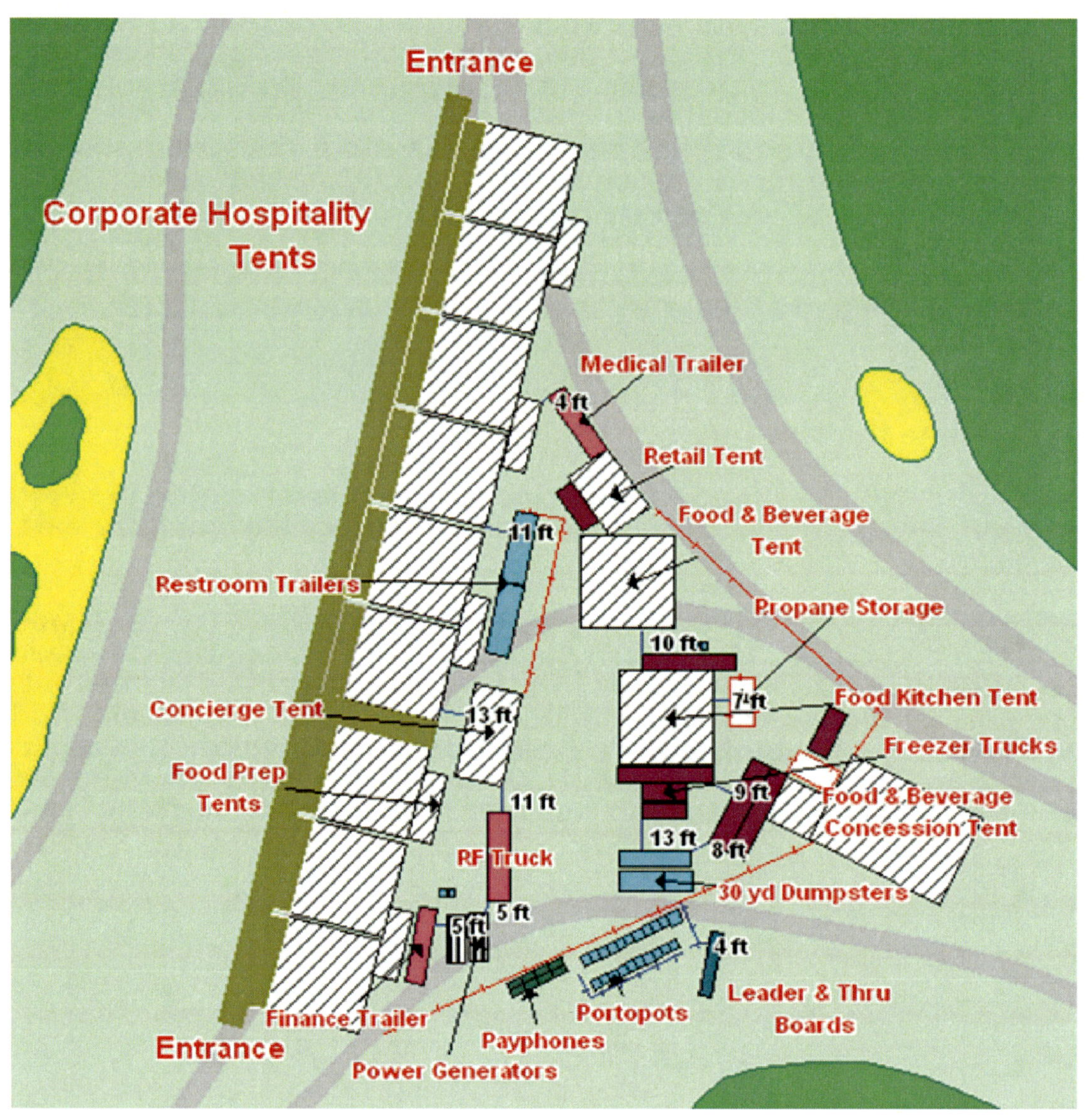

Chapter Four

Construction

This area has the potential to cost quite a bit, depending upon what amendments need to be made to the site for your event. Probable large ticket expense items are temporary roads, bridges, scoreboards, rental equipment, vehicles such as pick-up trucks and fork-lifts, containers, and tools.

The largest expense would most likely be the construction of temporary roads. Unless your event takes place on asphalt or has a cart path network throughout the site, or a permanent bus unloading area, you will probably have to construct some kind of road system on site.

This is not only necessary for access to important areas during the event, but also for the initial setup of facilities. For example, if there is a group of portopots in the middle of the course next to a concession, there would be no way to pump out the portopots, due to the size and weight of the truck necessary to do the job.

The old adage of "pay me now or pay me later" comes into play. You can roll the dice that there will be no rain during the time you are setting up, or during the event, or during tear-down.

You can hope the ground will remain hard. But unless your event is of the size that you can set up in one day, have the event and tear it out the next, you can probably count on some rain during the process. Heavy equipment and soft ground do not mix well. The costs for repair after the event might be more than building the necessary roads.

It is not necessary that these roads be concrete or asphalt. They may be composed of rock laid on top of a filter cloth fabric which can be removed after the event. Highway grade filter cloth is laid prior to spreading the rock to prevent the rock from being pushed into the ground when rolled with a compactor.

If the rock is pushed into the ground, it is a nightmare to remove it from the ground. Nevertheless, it will need to be removed, as you have to return the ground to the condition you found it.

Before roads are built behind the corporate tents, make sure the measurement from the tents to the road is correct and accurate. If it isn't, you will have to come back later and move the road because the tents are sitting on it.

Also, if you are putting roads over manholes, you will need to raise the covers to the height of the road for future access.

If the event is one that will be repeated in the same location for a number of years, you might want to consider asphalt. New materials come onto the market all the time so be on the lookout. There is a plastic mat system which shows a great deal of potential, but the costs are more than rock and less than asphalt at this time.

That being said, there is less damage to the ground with the mat system. There will be some compression with the mats, but they are much easier to install and pull up than rock or asphalt.

If the event is going to be in a northern climate, look to install the roads in the fall if possible. Over the winter, the rock will freeze and compress a few times, making it bind together better in the spring.

Another good reason to build the roads prior to spring is the amount of rain and the frost thawing associated with the spring months. Roads can't be built in the rain, and if you wait until weather subsides, there may not be enough time left to build the roads needed for the construction of the facilities.

If the ground is soft, no amount of filter cloth in the world will stop the rock from being pushed into the ground.

Equipment will be required on site during your event if you have rock roads. Depending upon the type of use, weight of vehicles, frequency of use, and the depth of rock installed, it may be necessary to rework the rock areas during the event.

This is because the ground beneath the rock may retain moisture, which will make roads become spongy and break down over time. Six by ten foot traffic plates may need to be on hand if the road breaks down on the bus loop during the peak operation.

These metal plates can be used to cover the trouble spots. When 200 full-size buses run 12 hours a day over the same rock road, unless the ground under the road is very hard, it most likely will experience deterioration of the road surface during the event.

When you are considering construction, consider the possibility of moving earth. This might be necessary if the ground where you want to install the corporate tents has too many rolling hills, Don't forget, you pay for the height of the floor, so if you can get level ground or, at least close to level ground, it will save a great deal of money. Three days at $1,200 a day to hire earth movers might save $10,000 in additional flooring costs.

Temporary bridges may be necessary to provide a safe walkway for the contestants trying to avoid areas congested with spectators. These locations are not always evident, but be alert to catch the locations early. At one event, a temporary bridge was constructed overnight, at great cost, to relieve the bottleneck created with the players and spectators. Bridges may be also necessary for providing spectator access to a site, possibly even crossing a highway. Each site is different, and these challenges should be discovered and identified during the site review.

Many of the areas of a golf event, for example, require scoreboards. On a golf course, leaderboards and thru boards are erected. Leaderboards are typically on every hole, to show where the leaders at that time and the thru boards, which are on every hole except the first, show the score of the group playing up to that hole. In the past, the scoreboard frames or catwalks were built out of wood or scaffolding and then magnetic boards were hung to a four by four foot back frame. Normally, on the 18th fairway adjacent to the green is the Monster Board, which is 27′ long by 18′ high and is mounted to I-beams. Concrete footers 3′ in diameter and eight feet deep are poured and the I-beams are attached to the footers. The board is designed to withstand 75 mph winds, not that I would ever want to test it.

Over the past few years, the Monster Board has been erected on temporary scaffolding, saving thousands of dollars by omitting the concrete footer costs. This should remind you to always be on the lookout for new ways to achieve the results you are looking for.

The public board is normally constructed out of wood and visually lists all of the player's scores for the week. It is constructed with four by four foot posts and plywood with a shake roof. The cost and design may vary with the taste of the event.

At some events, electronic scoreboards are used throughout the courses. These are powered by 12 volt car batteries.

Equipment needs fall into many categories. Heavy equipment encompasses fork lifts, genie lifts and bobcat steer loaders. Forklifts are necessary for the unloading of trucks and to move assorted material around, and are available in a variety of sizes. It is generally easier to rent at least one, to avoid having to wait to borrow one. Make sure a 4-wheel drive is rented. Two wheel drive forklifts will have trouble on wet grass or mud. Genie lifts are used to install televisions in the high cubes constructed above seating areas for easy viewing.

The picture below represents a straight mast, 4-wheel drive forklift. The picture on the right represents a boom lift forklift. The boom lift forklifts are invaluable for reaching high places, such as decks constructed high in the air.

Bobcats, shown below, can come with a variety of attachments, but the ones used most often are dirt buckets and augers. With the dirt bucket you can move mulch around or spread rock for walkways or paths, and the auger is vital for placing signs throughout the site.

Other rental equipment includes traffic cones and barricades, necessary to block off work areas. People tend to park in the wrong areas at the most inopportune times, so it is easier to block them off in advance. You might even need water-filled barricades to protect sensitive equipment from damage, as they can stop a car or truck.

Even if you have solidified a deal with a car rental company, chances are that vans and pickup trucks will still be needed, especially during crunch time. By the way, crunch time is the last week before the event. You'll need a few box trucks to move programs and televisions to their final destinations. These will alleviate the worry of rain prior to the event. Have a wide assortment of tools available for the operations crew, including compressors, paint guns, hand trucks, wire snips, an overabundance of plastic ties, and a good sense of humor. We'll talk about that later.

Eight by twenty foot or forty foot containers will be needed to store equipment and supplies.

These containers are used as a distribution point for programs, tools, trash boxes and bags, and a wide assortment of other things. Make a list, as each site is different and will have varying needs.

Golf carts may be a large expense, and if possible, a barter arrangement may be most advantageous. The number of carts necessary during the event for committee purposes is inconsequential, in comparison to the number needed for your vendors two months before the event, through the event, and up to two weeks following.

Vendor carts normally have four or six foot beds on the back, are gas powered for efficiency, and are very sturdy. These vehicles are worked long and hard, often carrying heavy materials. Flat tires and broken down carts are a constant battle. You should have a cart repair service person on site at least two to three times a week, to repair golf carts, whether it is flat tires or something more serious. Carts are a necessary evil in tournament operations.

Sometimes the club will get equipment donated for the event. Try to add three or four Gator carts to the deal, as they are much stronger and can handle more material. Gator is a brand name of a powerful, 4-wheel drive cart.

****

Now that you have fork lifts, bobcats and gas carts, fuel is a requirement.

If you're lucky, establish a deal with the club to use their gas pumps and pay them directly for the fuel. It is imperative to arrange a schedule for fuelling vehicles. Course maintenance crew's normal operation can't be interrupted. Close coordination with the superintendent is the key. It takes a lot of fuel to keep the operation humming smoothly.

If fuelling arrangements can't be coordinated with the club for whatever reason, a few portable 500 gallon tanks may need to be installed. The fire marshal will provide direction as to the best location. Fuel tanks will need to be protected from impact from heavy equipment by using concrete barriers or water-filled barricades. Also, an accounting system needs to be established to assist in tracking the correct allocations of fuel.

There are new systems available from your fuel provider, which are card readers to account for the fuel used by your vendors. Just assign a card to each vendor and there is no question concerning the amount of fuel used by that vendor.

In a previous chapter, flooring has been discussed, but there is more to consider. Using level flooring will provide many benefits to guests. It requires expertise to install, so make sure a vendor who is experienced handles the installation.

Remember, tents which are installed on top of the floor may be required by the building department to insure that the weight of the tent and number of occupants can be supported by the floor.

The flooring vendor needs to install the flooring efficiently and quickly. Have frequent meetings with the tent and flooring vendors to insure all the timelines are in sync and the completion date is accurate. If the floor isn't ready, the tents can't be installed. It's that simple.

Generally, tents need to be completed three to four days prior to the event, to allow the corporate clients to approve their tent layout. But it is also necessary to have time for the final touches, like the last bit of paint or landscaping.

You may choose to have a network of decked paths in the corporate villages or in front of concessions to help ease the potentially muddy conditions caused by rain. The natural ground deteriorates quickly when a lot of people are stomping on it. Flooring alleviates this problem.

Take into consideration, however, that if a wood deck path around a corporate village is installed and you need a rock access road for support behind the tents, you will have to have the deck stop at the edge of the road and then continue on the other side of the road, unless you want the trucks to crush the floor.

Bartering opens up a lot of discussion. Every event tries to trade for needed equipment and supplies. Hopefully, your event is strong enough to have a demand for tickets or some other items. If people want to be at your event because of the venue or the event has been sold out, then tickets are worth a great deal in trade.

Necessary items, such as television sets, copiers and faxes, vehicles, rental equipment, radios, generators, portable restrooms, restroom trailers, bottled water, lockers, flags and banners, landscaping, and furniture might all have trade value if the dollar amounts are high enough to be worth trading for tickets.

The number of tickets you can trade depends upon your event and the policies set. The cost of some of the items you need may so high that you may need to trade a hospitality venue to accommodate a fair trade value. Some events trade on-site advertising or signage. In tennis, the center court is the location that receives most television coverage. You might be inclined to sell the space on the tee markers for a golf event; car displays are not uncommon at others.

Space for a vendor to display product is another way to trade, value for value. Not all events are the same. Some don't allow any advertising whatsoever; others will sell space for anything with a value. Allowing trade is a business decision based on sources of revenue and level of expenses incurred.

When the printed program deal is structured, reserve a number of pages to trade for items of equal value. At times you will need to be creative to get what you need for the event. There is really no right or wrong way for bartering, but don't allow the site look-like a circus. You need to maintain some decorum while reaching your goals.
The items to be traded should be determined well in advance of the event, so that there is time to structure the right deals.

A Temporary road is shown in blue with the dimensions. It is necessary to access the concession and portopots for servicing and restocking.

As you create temporary roads on a site, the pertinent information can be entered into a database. This database will be extremely helpful when you are ready to write the construction requirements for the site.

This data is input for each proposed temporary road. It shows the length, width and depth of the road and the type of surface used. From this information, you can determine the square footage and cubic yardage of the surface necessary for the roads. It is a helpful tool when receiving construction bids in order to cross-check the calculations of your vendor.

Location	Depth	Width	Length	SF	CY	Type
1E	9	150	280	44,090	1,225	Rock
12E	9	16	1130	13,640	502	Rock
16E	9	16	1020	12,800	356	Rock
8E	9	16	140	2,560	72	Rock
Driving Range	9	16	740	11,840	330	Rock
4E	9	16	170	2,720	76	Rock
4E	9	180	1100	197,100	5,500	Rock
4E	9	16	330	5,280	147	Rock
4E	9	16	200	3,200	89	Rock

Chapter Five

Building Department

The building department can either be an ally or an opponent. It is always best to meet with the building department about your event early in the planning process.

That is worth repeating. It is always better to meet with the building department for your event sooner, rather than later.

Each area of the country is different, and each building department has its' own set of rules. While standard building codes exist, there can be codes specific to the local building department, and it is better to be familiar with these at the outset. Pay particular attention to the building codes with regard to tent spacing. In some locales you have to provide a fire break after a specific square footage or number of tents in a row. You will need to know this before you sign off on the tent layout.

The building department should communicate its expectations. Talk to them about the site and what you plan to do. Take maps to leave with them. Have a meeting with all the department heads; create an agenda that explains the scope of the event. Ask help in making your event painless for everyone.

During the practice rounds at one event, the building inspector came up to me and told me I had to move some tents in a corporate village. I knew the plans which had been submitted well in advance which should have uncovered the problem which was raised. Upon further review at the building department, the inspector found the plans were submitted, but no one caught the spacing issue. In the end, no tents were moved. This reinforces the fact that even if you begin early, errors will occur.

If it is your fault, you will need to ask the building inspectors for options. In almost all cases, something can be done to work around the problem. It may cost you money to solve the problem by either adding additional fire personnel or fire equipment.

The occupancy loads and the safety packages required for each tent should be known in advance and posted in the tents. A contingency plan should be written to accommodate all the people in the event of rain. Weather warning signs come out early enough to give notice of an impending storm, and that the spectators are urged to leave. You tell them the buses are lined up when the warning signs go up to move the people out. In the event of lightning on the course, you will open up all the tents, even corporate, to provide a temporary haven from the weather. Be careful here. It may be misunderstood that if there is a rain storm with no lightning the corporate tents would be open to the spectators. This is not the case.

I have always asked the question to the Fire Marshal: will you overload the occupancy of a tent during a lightning storm, knowing that structurally the floor and tent can handle it, or would you make the people stand in the lightning storm? I have never received an answer, and we have been lucky enough to have missed those storms. There isn't a tent big enough at any outdoor event to accommodate the masses in a rain storm, but the Fire Marshal will want to hear your plan.

They will also want to know what you are doing about medical services during the event, and the number of toilet facilities.The building department will want structural drawings of bleachers and possibly some tents, formally approved by a state licensed structural engineer: inspections will be made to insure plans are in compliance. It is not wise to play games with the building department and Fire Marshal. They are covering their jobs, as should you.

The American Disabilities Act (ADA) has finally made its rounds to outdoor special events. Ramps and walkways need to be ADA compliant. In fact, any place the general public can access needs to be ADA compliant. Designated viewing areas for spectators in wheel chairs or scooters must be provided. Concession areas and any tents that have counters should have counter heights that are wheelchair accessible. Obviously, there is nothing you can do about the ground conditions; after all, it is a golf course, but the more you can provide access, the more favorable experience it will be for disabled spectators.

Public payphones will need to be at the correct height, some will need to be TTD , telephones for hearing impaired, as well. There needs to be a number of wheelchair-accessible portopots throughout the course, also.

An arrangement may be made with a scooter company to provide a number of scooters for your disabled spectators. In addition, six-passenger golf carts may be procured to assist moving disabled spectators to a desired location to watch golf.

Wheelchair-accessible vans should be provided in the parking lots to transport wheelchair-bound spectators to the event.

Disabled access provisions should be widely communicated in pre-event publicity. Make sure the media relations department is aware of facilities are available for disabled spectators.

We will go into greater depth concerning ADA in Chapter 17.

When the event rolls around, expect some building department officials to attend; plan accordingly by providing credentials for them, as well as a limited number of parking passes to access the site. Parking is always a challenge, and they will understand this if it is explained in advance.

The Fire Marshal will want to see the flame certificates for the tents, as well as a list of hazardous materials used by the decorating company. This list might include the type of wood used in the walls or counters, the ceiling liner material, hard walls, stage lighting, and paint. A map showing the location of all these items should also be prepared and provided for quick review, in the event something should happen.

A golf cart should be provided for site access during daily inspections. It may also be required to provide a specially fitted cart with fire extinguishers and a 250-gallon water tank with hose attached. If necessary, this specially equipped cart may be rented through a number of vendors. Cities which are used to hosting events will in all probability own a few carts of this nature.

Potable water will be needed at various locations throughout the site and the code requirements for testing will be under the auspices of the health department. This will be discussed under ecology in Chapter 12.

This illustration shows placement of hazardous materials. The Fire Marshal will want a map showing all of the locations of hazardous material. In this particular case, the propane tanks needed for the food concessions are illustrated. Other hazardous materials would include generator placement, fuel tanks, and flammable materials.

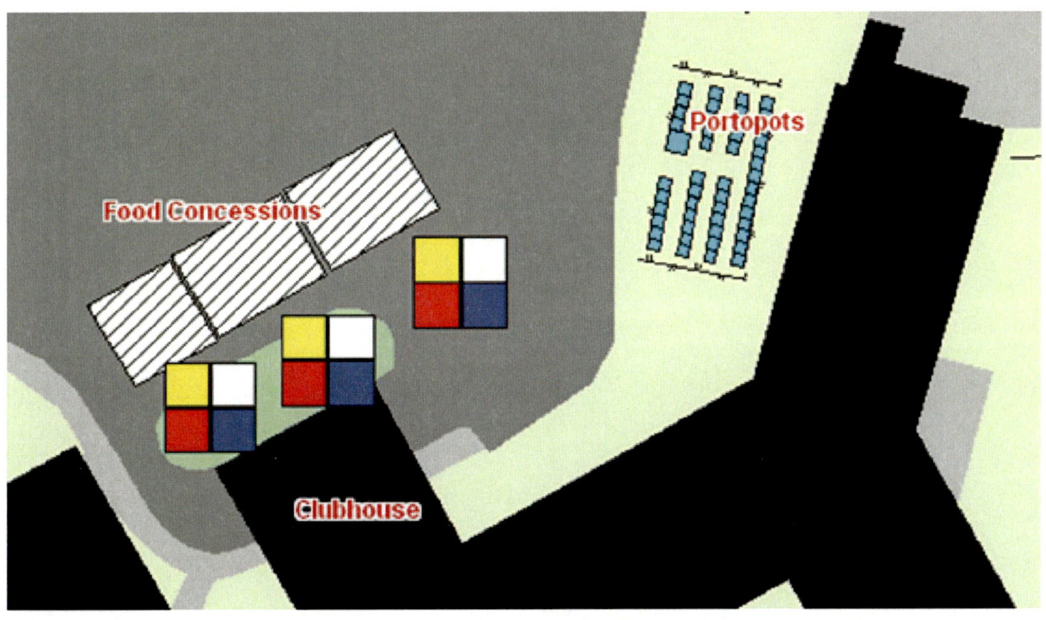

Chapter Six

Vendors

Selection of vendors is critical to the overall success of the event. You rely on your vendors and you are a team, or at least you had better be a team, or you will never finish on time. If you have bickering amongst vendors, a recipe for disaster is brewing. I have been blessed with exceptional vendors because I have worked at it.

Before picking vendors, find out who the decision maker is for the company. Deal directly with this individual. Define each area of the project and create a scope of work. The scope of work is then bid out to potential vendors. You need to verify that each vendor being considered has the experience to complete the job on time and without cost overruns. Most additional costs will be charged to the event in most circumstances. Of course, there will be things you forgot or items which will need to be changed, to accommodate the fluid nature of special events.

One thing you do have control over is the scope of work. When outlining scope, estimated equipment to be provided at no cost to the vendor, potential union issues, and items of a similar nature will be outlined in the contract. Make sure that all costs are included, even if you don't think they will apply. For instance, ask for the cost for pipe and drape, even though you think you will never need it. Having these costs at your fingertips will facilitate production of an accurate budget.

Because vendors have been selected based upon expertise and a long history of working events, you will find that they are a wealth of information. Often experienced vendors take your concept and find a way to build it, refine it or even improve it.

Don't be afraid to ask questions; it may save money in the long run. Some of these things will be discussed in later chapters.

Everyone has their own style when it comes to negotiations. Two people in the room playing "good cop, bad cop" is one of many strategies. This is when one person is constantly trying to drive the price down and the other is more lenient.

Another style is humor. By keeping the negotiations light, everyone is relaxed and humor is used to make points subtly. For instance, when the vendor in the room gives you a price which you know is inflated, you might say "I'm not trying to buy the company, I only want to rent it" or "I don't mind you making a profit, just don't make it on us." This will get the vendors' attention and make them rethink the pricing, but it won't create hard feelings. Your goal is to get the best possible price for the event's needs.

In some negotiations, the person on the other side of the bargaining table may take a hard line approach. If you can't soften them up, you will have to decide whether you need to also take a hard line approach. The vendor wants your business. It depends how much he wants your business. If it gets to a point that no progress is being made, you may have to say that you are at an impasse, and either walk away or schedule another meeting with the vendor. Then regroup and try again. If you still are at an impasse, you walk away . . . for good.

During the negotiation process, it is essential that you know that your superiors are backing you fully. Without this support, you may negotiate a good deal, only to have your superiors renege on the deal, making you look foolish. The point is to make sure your superiors are aware of planned strategies and actions.

In some areas of the country, unions are very strong and will make their presence known prior to your event. Being a good neighbor, you are willing to negotiate a number of higher-paid union personnel to work alongside your non-union vendors, although you are certainly under no obligation to do so. If the number of workers and budget can handle the additional expense, that's ideal. However, if one of the building trades decides they don't like the original deal and demands more, a decision must be made. You should have already discussed crossing picket lines with your vendors, but will these picket lines be a disruption to the event? You will have to make a tough decision.

More on Unions in Chapter 7: Living on the Edge.

Vendors will have been selected based upon criteria you established, whether it is cost and experience, or cost or simply experience. Just know that the least expensive vendor is not always the best vendor.

Over the years, we have signed multi-year contracts with certain vendors to gain a better price structure, as well as to provide continuity for the event.

There is an appendix in the back of the book with contact names and addresses.

The current tent vendor is Classic Tents. They have provided all the tents for us since 2008. It helps to establish this long-term relationship, as your expectations and areas of concern will already be known. They have also been adept on solving problems dealing with floor elevations and the needed ADA ramps.

Since 2005, the generator and HVAC vendor has been Aggreko. Over the years, they have been able to plan power and air conditioning needs as the event has grown larger. New products have reduced our footprint behind the house.

We have relied on Barton G for the look of the event, the design of banners, and the tent décor packages. His expertise and cutting edge creative ideas are known throughout the golf industry.

MSG Promotions has been given the task of selling all the corporate hospitality since 2004, a daunting task as the economy has shifted over the last five years. Changing economics has necessitated the need to research other avenues of corporate hospitality revenue. MSG has been able to stay ahead of the times and the corporate planners know they are getting straight answers from this group.

Ridgewells Catering has served our high-end catering needs since 1993 and over time has grown with the event.

Corporate clients feel comfortable seeing the same faces year after year and expect a high level of menus and service.

Prom has provided expertise and concession stand operations since 2000. They have developed menus which are specific to the geographic areas of the country where the championship is held. They have perfected the labor to operate the 14-16 concessions with few glitches.

Levy Catering has also proved to be a very reliable player with the food concession industry

In 2007, we hired Joan Stein LLC. a consulting firm to assist with ADA issues. We will discuss ADA in Chapter 17.

API has been involved with every event I've done since 1993. They have provided

all the cabling, installation of television dishes, and television channels necessary for the event. Their coordination of the receiving, distribution, and removal of all the televisions has been invaluable. Once they have the plan, they are self-sufficient and just get it done.

We have been lucky to have Clarence Davids to provide the coordination and installation of all of the landscape needed since 2003. They are one of the vendors that are low
maintenance and go about their business to create a wonderful look.

Elchik Builders out of Pittsburgh has been coordinating our carpentry needs since 2007. I developed a railing system that uses scaffolding posts secured to the framework of the tent substructure for stability, with wood inserts over the frames to produce beautiful, structurally sound railings. This is another example of a vendor who knows what your needs are and how to meet them in a first-rate fashion.

It will be imperative to include a zero tolerance policy for anyone drinking alcohol or using drugs on the site for any of your employees or vendors. This is worth repeating.

There is zero tolerance for employees or vendors to drink alcohol or use drugs on the site at any time.

The main reason is obviously the liability should something happen on site. Secondary reasons are creating a bad image for the venue, and the event's lack of control over the staff, and the accidents which may occur.

Major vendors, because their role and scope is so large, will require bigger compound space, and the smaller vendors will require much less.

Being creative with limited space is like putting together jigsaw puzzles. I have had sites so tight that there were compounds on top of compounds. On occasion, I've placed a vendor in an area because I knew they would be finished by the time the space was needed for another vendor who arrived later. It puts pressure on the first vendor to finish before being displaced from the space. At times you need to find creative ways .... and a bit of magic to get the job done.

Each vendor is going to need compound space, which was mentioned in the site review chapter. The tent contractor will need somewhere in the neighborhood of 38,000 square feet of compound space which should be ample enough to load and unload trucks, as well as have enough room for the storage of materials. Naturally, this also is based upon the size of the event. The vendor could erect a storage tent to keep some equipment out of the weather and a dining tent to feed their employees, which would require potable water. Make sure to have enough portable toilets available for employee use.

As the various venues are being constructed, vendors will find that they will move some of the toilets to the locations where they are working, to minimize the travel time and to keep the job on schedule. Make sure you tell the company servicing the portable toilets where the units were moved. Otherwise, the vendor won't know where they are, and the units will never be serviced.

Not good.

Take into consideration while planning compound space that some trucks can be off loaded in the areas where the work is being done, to cut down on the number of times the supplies need to be moved. Precision planning reduces the need to wait

for materials to be delivered. However, it could also cause a need for a storage area at that location.

Wood to be used in flooring systems will take up a huge amount of space. It is advantageous to have areas set aside for its storage adjacent to the areas requiring the flooring. In a perfect world, all the vendors would have all the space they could possibly want, but it is doubtful that will happen often.

The electrical and HVAC vendor are normally the same so their space can be combined. The electrical supplies are often stored in the compound and the HVAC trucks are normally off loaded in the areas where needed. The compound space should be around 25,000 square feet, which allows the vendor to spread out the electrical supplies by type and provides storage of additional air conditioning units. If your site does not accommodate the unloading of materials where they are to be used, the compound space must be increased to handle this need.

Don't forget that most vendors will have pickup trucks as well as golf carts to move equipment and transport employees. These vehicles, as well as heavy equipment must fit into individual compounds.

The media compound is typically a large area, as it includes a tent structure for the working media, an interview tent, dining tent, food prep tent and storage area, photographers' lounge tent, restroom trailers, and support trailers. This space is generally no less than 55,000 square feet combined. The tents should be in direct proximity to one another; other media facilities can be in the general vicinity.

The décor vendor, if one is retained, will require anywhere from 30,000 to 50,000 square feet, depending upon the size of the job. It is really based upon whether the work will be produced on site or shipped in from another location. If the work is going to be shipped in, it is normally trucked to the location where it will be installed, thus the need for compound space. However, until the corporate clients decide what kind of décor will be in their tents, the amount of space needed can't be determined. The décor company will generally have a production area, paint area, dining, and storage. In some cases, potable water will be needed for their operation.

The operations compound has grown over the years as the crew's responsibility has increased. The space required is approximately 15,000 square feet, which allows the placement of storage containers, painting areas, and a holding area for delivered materials. It will also contain a few office trailers from which the operations crew can operate and store tools. Pick-up trucks and heavy equipment will occupy a good amount of space. There should be at least a 20 x 20 foot tent somewhere in the compound to protect the crew from the elements while working.

Operations staffing will be discussed in a subsequent chapter.

Catering compounds have also grown over the years, due to the magnitude of the events being staged. Instead of having everything contained within the compound, trucks are being added to each location they are serving, to minimize the travel time from the compound. In the past, everything would have had to come from the main compound. The catering compound will vary from 31,000 to 50,000 square feet, depending upon the number and size of the tents to be serviced. Wedged in this compound will be the kitchen tent, a large number of refrigerated and dry storage trailers, loading docks, potable water, waste tanks, propane tanks, and warehouse, with additional storage trailers and loading docks. There is huge delivery area where tractor trailers can turn around to back up to the loading docks.

There will be a dining tent for employees and the office trailer, restroom trailer, and a human resource trailer. High speed data lines are essential for tracking inventory and to communicate with outlying areas and headquarters. Caterers are typically masters of space utilization.

The concessions compound is the most flexible. If there is not enough room on site, this compound can be located off site, although close by. The space requirements vary from 16,000 to 34,000 square feet, again depending upon the number and size of concessions throughout the site. Concession operators are self-sufficient during the day, restocking their tents at night.

The merchandise operation also requires a large amount of space, based upon the

size of the tent. The total space hovers around 64,000 square feet and includes an area for up to 22 storage trucks, loading docks, finance trailer, credit card transaction trailer, volunteer trailer, restroom trailer, and a volunteer tent.

However, they prefer to have a propane storage area on site, which sometimes causes headaches for you and the Fire Marshal. The compound normally requires ample room for delivery trucks backing into a loading dock to off-load into their storage trailers.

There must be room for a cardboard compactor and a dumpster. Somewhere in this area, the chillers for the air conditioning and the generators to provide the power need to find a home.

The television network compound has taken on a life of its own. For a small event, the compound will be nowhere near the size of 91,000 to 125,000 square feet currently required by a national broadcast network, supplementing an international feed. This area houses all the networks, which at last count totaled nine, including foreign broadcasters.

Not only do the production trucks need to fit into this space, but also restrooms, dining tents, 120 golf carts, two twin pack generators, communications, heavy equipment, 15 office trailers, uplink trucks, and hopefully some parking for personnel. This compound needs to be on the course, or at least adjacent to it.

The bleacher compound does not seem to vary much, and this vendor will use as much space as given, as they like to spread out their material. Generally speaking, 15,000 square feet works well. Unfortunately, almost all of the equipment needs to be dropped into their compound before it goes to each location for construction. The steel usually comes from a number of different jobs, so it would be difficult to load site-specific trucks. The compound needs to be big enough to turn large trucks around and accommodate an office trailer and heavy equipment. This area will need to have a stabilized surface, due to the amount of forklift traffic necessary to load and unload equipment.

The caddie compound, equipment repair vans, and the fitness trailers can all fit together in about a 14,000 square feet area. The items can be split up into smaller compounds, but the players will need safe access to the areas.

All of the compounds should be enclosed with fencing, to protect the vendors from unwanted guests. As the compound space for all the vendors is reviewed and plotted, remember that each one will need a power source. Shore power, the service you would receive from the local electric company, is the most preferred source, but not real feasible on a golf course, unless the event site will be permanent and you have the ability to install transformers in all the areas needed.

In most cases, the power sources will be generators of various sizes and will need to be sound attenuated. This means you can stand next to the generators and carry on a normal conversation. These generators will occupy a lot of space, whether in compounds or at tent locations. Consider grouping some facilities to cut down on the number of generators necessary.

The fueling of all generators is paramount to avoid inopportune shutdowns. Select a fueling vendor large enough to handle this immense job. This is normally coordinated through your electrical vendor. It would be advantageous to create a map depicting the locations of all the generators.

Extra fuel tanks should be provided for the generators that run through the fuel faster than others. One of the most infuriating things that occurs at any event during setup, when everyone is working at a frenetic pace, is the truck driver who shows up with a load of material and no clue as to whom or where it is to be delivered. Hours can be wasted attempting to identify and track down the correct vendor.

It is absolutely imperative that you stress to ALL of your vendors the importance of the correct shipping and receiving instructions for the site. All truckers should have the contact name, phone number and company name of the vendor to which the materials are being delivered. There is no such thing as too much information on the label or bill of lading. Boxes get lost simply because no one knows where they are supposed to be delivered.

Due to most sites being so compact, it may be wise to have an offsite staging area for big trucks with deliveries. They can call the appropriate vendor once they have reached the area, and the vendor can lead them onto the site, causing the least amount of disruption to other vendors . This has worked very well in the past.

A week to ten days prior to the event, a package distribution person should come on site to manage the responsibility involving carriers such as Ups and Fed Ex. This is normally a paid position, and all packages will be received by their staff and distributed to the right people on a timely basis. It will alleviate twenty packages outside your office on a daily basis.

Package distribution will also be responsible for all shipping requests during and following the event. This service is invaluable, as it allows you to focus on other things. Package distribution will need a trailer, storage container, a small tent, and a few golf carts for distribution of packages.

Take the time to get to know your vendors. You need all of them to work as a team, and when one is having a problem, it can affect all of them. I spend a great deal of time in the mornings during setup, checking with every vendor to make sure they have everything they need from me. This might include additional maps; areas marked out, or information on what part of the site I want them to go next. At one event, the vendors put up a sign during construction, which read, "Welcome to Busseyville, Mayor Bussey Presiding." To me, it meant I was doing my job, by keeping everyone in the loop as to the schedule and solving small problems before they became huge problems.

The vendor routing map is passed along to all the vendors prior to the event. It is the vendors' responsibility to pass the routing map to their employees. On the map below, the different colored lines with arrows show the various preferred routes the vendors are to follow. These routes were discussed with the golf course superintendent and approved. The superintendent knows what areas hold water or where sensitive habitat areas might be.

As you can see on the map, the routes provide access everywhere the vendor will need to go. The colored line would reflect whether the area can be accessed by all vehicles or only golf carts.

Chapter Seven

LIVING ON THE EDGE

Unions

Not many people talk about unions out loud, or at least they never put the opinions in print. I have had a great deal of experience with unions, some good....some not so good.

In 2002, during the Open setup at Bethpage, the carpenters union paid me a visit, not quite what you have heard in the movies, but close. They wanted ALL the work at the US Open; it was their entitlement. I disagreed. And the journey began.

Bethpage is a state-run facility with a great deal of politics involved, so the thought of any disruption by the union rippled through the people in charge.

The union tried to play games and filed reports about workers and wages.

Every allegation the union made proved to be inaccurate, but the political people in charge wanted the situation to just go away, so I negotiated a settlement.

Once the carpenters union settled, then the machine operators, iron workers, HVAC, and stagehands all wanted a piece.

It didn't matter that we needed nobody from any group to make the Open run as we had for all the previous years, but here we were.

It took more labor to make sure the unions were working and more time for the job to get done, because the work was not something they had done every day and the amount of time for every break taken added up quickly.We limped through the setup, while paying close to $500,000 we would not normally have had to pay.

Jump forward to 2006 at Winged Foot in Mamaroneck, NY. It started out to be the same deal, but the president of the building trades this time was a forward thinker and understood our limitations. We hired the unions again, but used a smaller crew than before, and the men were hand-picked for the Open. Even though they didn't quite produce as much as the normal crews who do this every day, they worked hard and replaced those who were not pulling their weight.

It was a good relationship.

In 2009, when we came back to Bethpage, we reached out to the president of the building trades, the same person who worked with us in 2006 at Winged Foot. It could not have gone better. The number of people requested was reasonable and we could handle the costs. Again, the men who were sent to us were people who wanted to work, not the ones who wanted to cause trouble as happened previously.

Over the next three years, we used a smattering of union personnel, but nothing ever coming close to what was used in 2002 or 2006, until 2013 for the Open at Merion, near Philadelphia.

We met with the representative for the carpentry union in February 2013. I laid out what we would normally use for an event this size and he took the information back with him. Evidently my proposal was not what they wanted to hear, because they sent letters out to senators and every vendor telling them the Open was a union job and to stand down.

They did not respond directly to my proposal, but rather decided to picket and erect a large balloon rat figure to draw attention to themselves as construction started in late March. A few emails ensued and finally a meeting with the president of the carpenters union.

The meeting was not expected to go well, as the representatives had presented to him that the offer was one of disrespect, which was not the case.

The meeting was all about the union's right for all the work at the Open, meaning all the bleacher, tent and flooring construction. This was not something we would ever agree to, but the union had backed themselves into a corner, leaving very little room to negotiate... so there was a standoff.

As I said, the meeting did not go well, and we were to come back with another proposal.

In the interim, the picketing pressure was ramped up around the club, flyers were sent out with my email and phone number, which made for some interesting emails and phone messages.

During this three-day flurry, we were contacting all vendors to see who would cross a picket line during the Open. We needed to be sure that if this escalated through the Open, supplies still flow, especially food, beverage and sanitation.

As a side bar, I was have meetings with the stagehands, teamsters, and machine operations and signing agreements with them for their portions of the Open. Each of these groups was very reasonable.

Then meetings with the electrical union had begun, and it seemed like "deja vu," as they wanted all things electrical. After we told them we could give them some but not all, we were at a stalemate with them also.

We had set up another meeting with the carpenters union president. This was now early April, and there were more picketers at three locations around the club, being a general nuisance. This meeting took a different turn.

The president of the carpenters union walked away from involvement, leaving the entire negotiation to his son. I had been talking to the son on a regular basis, and once I had put the possibility of more work on the table beyond the original scope offered, their stance on needing all the work softened a little.

I continued to talk to the son every day; it was now April 9, and as each day went by, less work was available. On the 10th I had a verbal agreement on the scope of work I had written, but was still waiting for a signed copy. We received a copy of the signed agreement on the 11th of April.

On April 15, the carpenters union rejected my choice of a union subcontractor as my point person for all the union personnel, which would have helped me tremendously. As a result, I had to take on all the responsibility of chasing down the guys when they weren't doing what they were supposed to, as well as verifying their hours on a daily budget, keeping my eye on the "not to exceed" number... The union began work on the 16th.

Skipping down some to cover important points.... There was not a day that went by that the carpenters didn't push for more work, or said what other people were doing should be their scope.

They wandered around the site, searching others' business, trying to create more work for themselves that wasn't there. Each time I referred them back to the contract, but it was tiresome.

Let's go back to the electrical union, which really sat on the sideline until we worked out our deal with the carpenters. They were back and unyielding to what they wanted, which was unreasonable, and we were at a stalemate again.

Then we had a meeting with them and a senator. In this meeting, the attitude changed, they were willing to compromise, and a deal was struck. I will say the electrical union lived up to their word and did their job without any further trouble.

As we got closer to the Open, the carpenters union now wanted to discuss men for the tear down after the Open was over. We said it was off the table and never in the deal from the first day of all discussions. They didn't care. It was on the table now.

We compromised by giving them some standby work during the Open, which amounted to their guys sitting around doing nothing during the Open, as all the work had been completed. The other trades, stagehands, teamsters, and machine operators all did their jobs without complaining or pushing for more.

The Open ended and so did the involvement with the union.

These were the facts of my involvement with the unions for the past 21 years. As I said, depending on the size of the event and the amount of exposure (media coverage), you may have a few of the unions who want to be involved. If the economy is strong, in most cases, they will not bother with a small event.

It will always come down to what is reasonable. You will most likely have to give more than you want, and they will have to take less than what they want.

CHAPTER EIGHT

FEAR

One of the definitions of fear is to consider or anticipate (something unpleasant) with a feeling of dread or alarm

I wanted to mention how fear can impact running an event.

Anyone new in charge of a project or an entire event would understand the word fear.

It can be immobilizing, however it doesn't need to be. Decisions are made all the time and the difference between a leader and a follower is a leader is willing make decisions based upon the facts known. You will need to take responsibility if you are given an assignment. You own that assignment. It is yours to come up the procedures and timelines for the project, but not without asking tons of questions.

There should be no unclear areas.

If you have all the facts, go with it and make decisions. However, if there are items missing from your project or areas which this project could impact not having been considered, you aren't ready to make sound decisions.

The more informed you are about what you are asked to do the more complete job you can do. You supervisor will welcome the questions and appreciate the attention you are giving to assignments.

This is what will ultimately defines your abilities in operations.

People in operations are going to make mistakes because in most cases decisions need to be made quickly decisions quickly. In fact, in some cases the decisions need to made within seconds to avoid a potential disaster. There is no way around that. The more experience you have in events, any events, the better you will be prepared for impending catastrophes with the ability to minimize them. Don't let fear stop you from doing what you know is right.

I was working as a stadium manager years ago at Palm Beach Polo and Country Club when the players had finished the match they would ride to the center of the field in front of the 10,000 person packed stadium for the award ceremony. They would normally dismount and be handed wet and dry towels to clean their muddy faces from the dirt being kicked up during the match.

I was on my way to the locker room 5 minutes prior as usual to pick up the towels, put the key in the lock and turned. It only turned half way. The door didn't open.

So here you are...decision time...what do you do? Fear set in...what if you couldn't get the towels to the field? How would that make the company look on national television? I made the decision to kick in the door. As luck would have it, the President of the company walked by, saw what I was doing and probably thought I was crazy.

Later he understood my reasoning which was: it was more important for the players to have the towels for the award ceremony in front of thousands people than what it would cost replace a $150 door. Fear could have stopped me from

getting the job done but it didn't.

The president agreed, but as you can see, things can be deceiving. Not everything requires split second decisions, but you need to be prepared to act when it is required and then stand behind your decisions. What would you have done?

In another example years ago, I was running the operations for a women's professional tennis indoor circuit, and we were in the basement of a building in Princeton, New Jersey, setting up for a tennis match between Chris Evert and Martina Navratilova. It was a sellout crowd.

The Fire Marshal came up to me and said that the promoter had sold too many tickets and 300 people weren't going to be allowed to see the match.

I was the guy who had to tell these people who were lining the halls on the first floor. As I was going up in the elevator from the lower floor, I could feel a headache coming and a sense of dread. This is the fear I have been talking about. In this case there is nothing you can do about the situation except suck it up and deal with it.

Standing in the hall face to face with the angry mob, I proceeded to tell them the Fire Marshall had reduced the occupancy for the match and they wouldn't be able to see it. Their money would be refunded. Some had driven 100 miles to see this match, and I couldn't blame them for being upset. This was a very unpleasant experience, not one I have ever repeated since.

Lesson learned: Always check with the Fire Marshal for occupancy loads on anything you do; don't trust anyone else, so this doesn't happen to you. Keep in mind that you are training for these decisions during every event you do, large or small. Most people around you aren't trained for high pressure situations, so you will be looked upon to have the right answers and make the correct decisions. You can't let fear stop those decisions.

Keep in mind that you are training for these decisions during every event you do, large or small. Most people around you aren't trained for high pressure situations, so you will be looked upon to have the right answers and make the correct decisions. You can't let fear stop those decisions.

I must admit there have been times when there was no experience from which to draw, but common sense usually prevailed.

Start building that experience today.

There are other kinds of fear. For example, say you have made a mistake, and it's a big one in your eyes, and you need to inform your supervisor or vice president. That is when fear sets in.

The best thing you can do is to come clean immediately; don't try to hide it. State the facts. This will diffuse the situation immediately.

If your supervisor is a leader, he will show you where you went wrong and back you up to anyone else involved. In most cases, the magnitude of a mistake you have made is never as bad as you think it is.

That will be a mistake you will never make again. In one case, one of my operations supervisors was supposed to place the player club repair vans into an area. Unfortunately, this was a low lying area, and saturated with water, having rained the previous five days.

The correct thing to have done was to get sheets of plywood to lay on the ground to protect it, so the heavy trailers can drive on it with more stability.

The supervisor thought he could get the vehicles in if he moved quickly to minimize the damage to the grass.

Huge mistake.

The first truck took a run at the location and created trenches where the wheels traveled almost a foot deep and then came to a quick stop. It was just too wet to get traction.

When I was called and showed up, it was a real mess. The supervisor expected the worst from me, but he had just made a mistake. It was one that could be fixed with some grading of the trenches and addition of new sod. He could have been fearful when telling me what had happened, and that feeling would have been justified if I was the type of leader who yelled at everything instead of knowing my supervisor knew what he did and felt bad about it.

The rest of the trucks were placed on top of plywood.

Chapter Nine

TENTS AND FURNITURE

By this point, you have already done the site review and facility placement. The next topic is tents. To get the best pricing, it will be beneficial to commit your tent vendor to a long term contract of at least four years, providing you are operating several events. Make sure you review a number of reputable companies during this bidding process.

You will need to include every possible contingency to avoid last minute ordering, as invariably, there are associated costs. It will be helpful to maintain a spreadsheet outlining what has been ordered and the date. There are many tent varieties, ranging from pole, frame, and structure. Pole tents are passé for sporting events. Frame tents may be used for smaller events, but if you are trying to achieve a professional look and don't want rope and stakes holding tents down, you will want to consider structures.

This is an example of a tent village under construction. All of the tent framing is completed on the right side and the left side is half completed. The tents shown are structures.

This is an example of covering the understructure of the tents. In this picture, a product called T1-11 is being fastened to the scaffolding. Windscreen may also be used at a much reduced cost, but it depends upon the look you are trying to achieve.

Structures are more expensive but add a clean look to the event and are very strong. Depending upon the type of structure, there is a lot of usable space, and depending on what you are putting inside, you will need every square inch of usable space.

As you can see, the construction of the corporate villages is almost complete. The flooring is finished and the carpet is being installed. The landscape is installed next, along with the picket fence on the patios.

The larger tents are used for corporate table pavilions, merchandise, media, upgraded concessions and some special hospitality groups. Other structures may include on-course concessions, corporate hospitality tents, admissions canopies, and support tents, which will be seen by the spectators. The general rule to follow is: if the general spectator is going to see the facility, it needs to be a structure. This adds a visible continuity to the site, as opposed to having structures next to frame tents.

This is an example of the construction of one of the larger tents. It is six feet off the ground and is supported with scaffolding. Notice the beams under the floor where the tent leg base plates are located. This adds more support for the weight of the tent leg.

The back of the house is not so strict, and frame tents have been used in these areas on occasion. The tent material should be flame retardant and have the certificate attached to the tent for easy viewing by the Fire Marshal, who will look for it. It should also be clean, in like-new condition and free of any defects or holes. The sizes of tents used are dictated by the proposed use. You can't cram twenty people in a 10'x10' tent unless you're trying to set some kind of record, so you need to think about what you are trying to accomplish.

Structures are anchored to the ground using three foot long metal stakes. Structural straps are also attached to the corners of the large tents and aurgured into the ground.The back of the house is not so strict, and frame tents have been used in these areas on occasion. The tent material should be flame retardant and have the certificate attached to the tent for easy viewing by the Fire Marshal, who will look for it. It should also be clean, in like-new condition and free of any defects or holes. The sizes of tents used are dictated by the proposed use. You can't cram twenty people in a 10'x10' tent unless you're trying to set some kind of record, so you need to think about what you are trying to accomplish. Structures are anchored to the ground using three foot long metal stakes. Structural straps are also attached to the corners of the larger tents and augured into the ground.

In all probability, there will be food prep tents erected behind each corporate hospitality tent. You will need to make sure your tent vendor attaches a rain gutter between the main tent and the food prep, to divert any rain water away from the interior of both tents.

There also needs to be a method of diverting water from around all sides of the tents to insure the carpet and wall coverings do not become saturated with runoff from a rain storm. This is not an easy task, so pay special attention . . . trust me!

If you intend to hang banners or apply appliqués to the tent surfaces, you need to make sure that the tent vendor will allow it. There may be an additional charge to remove these items. The décor company and the tent company will need to work together cooperatively to coordinate the installation of these items.

It will be part of the tent vendor's contract to install the safety packages for each tent in accordance with state, county and local building codes. This will include all battery-powered exit signs and fire extinguishers deemed necessary by the fire marshal. Make sure you ask the fire marshal the type of fire extinguisher needed for each area. It will also be suggested that you provide urns filled with sand to extinguish smoking materials. Smoking materials tossed in the landscape have started fires and during dry conditions present a hazard.

Furnishing all areas can be a daunting task. You have to do your homework and decide the kinds of furniture needed. Office trailers where meetings are held should contain office furniture that reflects that function. You will need to determine the number of desks, side chairs, executive chairs, conference tables and filing cabinets needed for each upgraded area. You may need to provide computers in some areas. If this is the case, you may want to purchase these items as opposed to renting, as the costs may be the same.

The furniture for the support areas or areas around the course can be of the folding variety, as it will be used for only a week. You will choose from 4, 6, or 8 foot banquet tables for support groups to place equipment or supplies. In some cases you may need 48" or 60" round tables for dining tents. The tables will need to have some kind on material on the top and in some cases, skirting around the table to hide whatever is underneath.

Each event is different, and you have to weigh the costs and benefits associated with this area. Pay close attention to what each area of the event is requesting. In some cases it is warranted and in others, it isn't.

A spreadsheet for this area is vital. It is very easy to lose track of what has been ordered and the location where it is supposed to go. This would include each area: tents, trailers, or on-course. It would include the size of the table, topped with plastic or not, skirted or not. An example of the type of spreadsheet needed is included at the end of this chapter.

Needs are constantly changing, and an accurate spreadsheet should be revised often to keep the tent company up to date and to maintain your budget. Start early in determining your needs. You may have to interview each committee or create an order form, which can be filled out for your review. All requests must be in writing and signed appropriately.

Work out a delivery schedule for the furniture. The tent vendor has to pay its suppliers by the day, week, and month, and so will you. I caution you not to wait until crunch week, which is the week prior to the event. There will be too many things going on to give the proper attention to what is being delivered and where. Some areas will be missed, and you will not be able to maintain an accurate inventory of what you have ordered.

There are areas that will need longer lead time, such as office furniture. Be sure to plan for these areas well in advance. Office furniture is normally not provided by your tent vendor. The trailer vendor may provide this service or an outside office furniture rental company may be able to provide it.

Make sure to have staff available to escort the furniture to the right areas. This will save a tremendous amount of time trying to find the furniture guy when he invariably gets lost.

Pricing should be agreed upon well in advance, and contract pricing should include lost items. This will motivate the tent company to move swiftly after the event to remove all the tables and chairs from the tents and trailers. If that contract inclusion is not possible for your event, come to an agreement for the pricing of lost items. It should be the wholesale price of each item, not retail pricing, as you are not purchasing the item to keep, only renting it.

The schedule for picking up the furniture following the event should also be reflected in the agreement, to avoid any later misunderstandings.

If the tent vendor is not responsible for picking up the furniture after the event, you will need dedicated people to pick up all the tables and chairs. This task can take four people three to four days to accomplish. If you forget to plan for this, your staff will be overtaxed trying to catch up.

****

I remember one time when the tent vendor came up to me after the event and told me he was missing an inordinate amount of tables and chairs that he had subcontracted for the event. Since I knew the vendor well, I realized there had to be an explanation. There were too many tables and chairs missing to be stolen by other vendors, so I asked around. It turned out that the décor company had rented then from the same contractor as my tent vendor and were shipped to the new venue without the subcontractor telling the tent vendor. In other words, the subcontractor was trying to double dip on the rental and claim a huge loss for which I would have been liable. After all these years, not much surprises me.

Name	Location	Size	Sq.Ft.	Tent	Floor	Elevation	Elevation	Liner	Carpet	Turf	Doors	Fire	Storage		Total
				Price			Price					Ext			
Tent1	3rd Fair	10x10	100	200	0.25	0-2'	0	no	no	0.05	no	1	no		$280
														Total	

The above is an example of a typical spreadsheet to prepare and share with the tent vendor. It shows the name of the tent, location, size, square foot of the tent, tent price, floor price, elevation of the tent, and associated cost of the elevation. There are columns for tent ceiling liners, carpet or astro-turf, doors, fire extinguishers, storage units, and totals.

Instead of having a price showing for floor, you may choose to have a column for the total cost, including flooring up to that point. You could then add a "total" column after every category. How you set up the spreadsheet is according to personal preference. But it should make sense and easily readable.

Furniture	Size	Description	Quantity	Unit Price	Total
Tables	18"x8'	Conference	20		
Tables	60"	Round	19		
Tables	48"x30"	Banquet	30		
Tables	72"x30"	Banquet	108		
Tables	96"x30"	Banquet	282		
Tables	48"	Round	25		
Chairs		Samsonite Folding	1078		
Chairs		Banquet	973		
Chairs		White Wood	214		
Chairs		Plastic Patio	100		
Media Desk		Working Media	185		
Media Desk		Registration	2		
Media Desk		Photo Lounge	10		
				Total	

The furniture spreadsheet is very basic. You need to know the type of furniture delivered, size, description, quantity, and unit price to arrive at a total cost.

Information will be assembled from another spreadsheet that encompasses every area on the site. All the trailers and tents will need some type of furniture.

Furniture	Size	Description	Quantity	Unit Price	Total
Tables	18"x8'	Conference	20		
Tables	60"	Round	19		
Tables	48"x30"	Banquet	30		
Tables	72"x30"	Banquet	108		
Tables	96"x30"	Banquet	282		
Tables	48"	Round	25		
Chairs		Samsonite Folding	1078		
Chairs		Banquet	973		
Chairs		White Wood	214		
Chairs		Plastic Patio	100		
Media Desk		Working Media	185		
Media Desk		Registration	2		
Media Desk		Photo Lounge	10		
				Total	

Chapter Ten

TRAILERS

You will have a need for trailers of some type. Office trailers come in all kinds of styles, sizes, colors and conditions.

If you are constructing a building and you need a construction trailer, you aren't really going to care what it looks like, but at an event, if it is going to be visible, it will need to have a consistent appearance. From the outset, inform the vendor that you aren't going to accept trailers in disrepair. In all probability, you will not need the 110 trailers used for a major golf championship from year to year, but what you need should still be consistent in appearance.

Photos courtesy of GE's Modular Space

8'x24' Trailer   8'x32' Trailer

Office trailers generally come eight, ten or twelve feet wide and twenty-four, thirty-two, forty-eight and sixty feet long. Pricing is based upon the width and length and naturally, the time period during which it will be used. There are other associated costs, such as delivery, set-up and removal, as well as for steps or ramps to the doors. Some come with bathrooms, others don't; you will need to be specific in this process. It would be nice to have large trailers everywhere, but again it will be dictated by available space and proposed use.

If one 10' x 48' trailer can take the place of two 8' x 32' trailers, you might want to consider it. Be mindful of the fine print in the contracts you sign.

Photos courtesy of GE's Modular Space

10' X 44" TRAILER   12' X 60/ TRAILER

There is normally a cleaning charge per trailer, but this is typically negotiable. The reasoning is normally the trailers have to be cleaned before they are rented anyway, so maybe you can just pay for those that will be particularly messy.

The trailers need to be in good condition, unless they aren't going to be seen and you are putting construction vendors in them. You may need to inspect the trailers in the yard before they are shipped if you have any concerns.

Everything needs to work in the trailers; no broken outlets or air conditioning that doesn't work. Fixing these things on site will be a pain and time consuming. The exterior paint needs to be of a consistent color with other trailers on site, unless they won't be seen by spectators. If necessary, the company may need to come on site and repaint the trailer. I have had trailers painted at a number of events due to the condition they were in upon arrival.

Trailers at most events do not have the bathrooms hooked up, as it requires the additional expense of running water to the trailer and installing holding tanks that need to pumped periodically. Some trailers will need to have restroom facilities, depending upon the occupant or the length of contract.

If the trailers are only used for a week, then in most cases, the built-in restrooms can be used for additional storage. There are normally portable toilets in close proximity.

Every trailer ordered might not have the exact interior floor plan you need. You can have walls added or removed, but know that you may have to pay the trailer company to restore the trailer to its original configuration. You need to discuss this with the vendor in advance.

There may be trailers which are needed longer than a month, but most will fall into a month's rental. I would suggest that if you have need for trailers longer than a month that you consider the placement of these close to a shore power source or within a short distance from one. If you use generators in these locations, it becomes a maintenance issue, as well as typically a bit more expensive. You will need to fuel the generators, depending upon the load, every two or three days. Oil and fuel filters need to be changed periodically, requiring the generator to be shut down.

If you have a large event, additional consideration must be given to the delivery schedule of these trailers. It would be impossible to deliver 90 or 100 trailers, block and level, hook up power, phones and cable during a month's period. Work with your trailer vendor and develop a plan to accept delivery as soon as the trailers are available. The trailer vendor will normally work with you, as they understand the scope of this process. Since you are normally paying a one month's rental minimum, you will want all the trailers on-site at least one month prior to the event.

If your event is a one-time event, it may be difficult to get the lowest pricing. Depending upon the exposure for the trailer vendor, you may be able to negotiate reasonable pricing.

The delivery charges will vary, depending how far you are from the yard where the trailers are staged and whether there are restrictions as to the day and time the trailer vendor is allowed to travel. The post-event cleaning of the trailers and the installation of the steps for all the trailers is usually negotiable, but any trailer that is unusually dirty will incur a charge.

Depending upon the height of the trailers from the ground or its use, local building codes may require the trailers to have tie-downs. If this is the case, there will be an additional charge.

Ask your trailer vendor where they want you to drill holes in the trailers to install phone and television cable. Some companies don't care, others do. Make no modifications to any trailers without the consent of the trailer company, because you will be charged to put the trailer back to its original configuration and condition once the tournament is complete.

When placing trailers on your site, you will need to coordinate with the golf course superintendent and the club to determine when you will be allowed to begin placing trailers. There may be sensitive areas that will require you to wait until a certain date, unless it is vital to the immediate operation.

The routes to each location need to be determined. If the delivery requires driving on grass, then the ground will have to be dry to minimize the creation of ruts in the ground, or you will need to place sheets of plywood on the ground to act as a temporary road to minimize damage. I have had trailers sitting on the course for two weeks after the event due to rain. It would not be cost effective to install a rock road if you are only placing one or two trailers on the course. There were enough trailers to move which allowed these to sit until dry weather prevailed.

Depending upon how tight the location is, it may be necessary to relocate to another areas or possibly remove some trees.

At the end of the event, you will want to remove the most highly visible trailers first. It will be helpful to the trailer vendor if you provide a place where they can stage trailers for later removal. Make sure you remember where all the trailers were placed. At one event, it took the trailer company a month to find one missing trailer because it was buried in the trees to hide it from the public view.

The trailer vendor may remove one of the wheels on trailers eight by twenty-four feet or smaller once they are placed, to insure they won't disappear mysteriously after the event. These trailers are so small that they may be moved by a pick-up truck.

Storage trailers come with wheels or without, depending upon the use and the accessibility to the site. Those with wheels come in handy for the merchandise operations, as well as for the concessionaire and caterer for storage of dry goods.

Refrigerated trailers can also be ordered, but pay particular attention to the power requirements. Before ordering any trailers that have wheels, consider the use, as you may need to build loading docks, or at the very least, stairs. Make sure you have the room to build any loading docks you may need. You will also need to install lights in these trailers, unless you can see in the dark.

Storage trailers without wheels are commonly called containers, and they sit on the ground, hopefully level ground. These trailers can come in lengths of 20' or 40' and they also can be refrigerated. They provide the same use as the others, but would not require steps. However, they do arrive on a rather large truck that needs room to maneuver. If the maneuvering room is not available, you may need to rent a huge forklift to set them in place.

Chapter Eleven

ELECTRICAL AND HVAC

This is a vitally important area and not without its problems. These vendors have a huge
responsibility and a good deal of liability. When choosing these contractors, follow the same guidelines outlined for the tent vendor. First and foremost, make sure they have the ability to do the job on time and within budget. Check references or visit an event they are supplying and talk to the operations people.

Make sure that all the items are outlined and priced, so there are no surprises. The electrical side of any event has a lot of variables, but we'll break them down. The electrical in each tent needs to be separated into 208 volt circuits, or normal house current, which go back to panels that go back to the power source. The number of circuits is based upon the electrical needs or outlets for each tent.

Some additional circuits are usually held in abeyance for the "oops factor": I forgot this or that. You will need to have a large supply of power strips that have fuses, available for a number of devices that need to operate close to one another. Check with each client and support group to determine the number needed. It is usually more cost effective to buy the power strips directly from an outlet store instead of from your electrical contractor, but check first. The caterer will have special requirements for the food prep tents, and these items must be included in the power requirements to avoid exceeding maximum loads.

That takes care of the 208 volt power; now you have to consider the 408 volt power, which is what the air conditioning and heat run on. Once the overall electrical requirements for each tent have been established and the panels have been sized, the amount of power necessary to run the tent or groups of tents can be determined.

All cable should be UL approved, with color coded cam locks for safety. The color codes on the cam locks make it easy for the installer to know which connections go where. They simply match the colors. The electrical inspector will want to meet with the electrical contractor to inspect all connections to the power source. There will be few problems with the inspections, as long as the directions from the building department are followed from the outset.

This is an example of a typical power distribution panel.

Photo provided by Aggreko

This vendor may also be responsible for the lights in most of the tents, as well as plugging in all the televisions in the corporate areas. Regardless of whether the tent or electrical vendor is providing the basic lighting, there will invariably be a need for upgraded lighting somewhere. This might be as simple as additional general lighting or as extensive as stage spot lights.

These lights need to be included in the electrical specifications, as they tend to increase the power loads substantially, and, in some cases, even the panel size.

In addition, you may contract with the same vendor to place the light towers in the locations you need and supervise their fueling. Light towers will be necessary in any area spectators will be walking after dark, as well as in each vendor compound. Light towers typically have a self-contained generator, with a four light boom that can be raised up to 20 feet and aimed in the direction needed.

The number necessary will vary per event, but don't forget to include the remote parking areas, as the shuttle system will depend upon the lighting if buses are being loaded in the early morning. If you have contract security in these areas, put in their contract that one of their duties will be to start the light towers at dusk and turn them off in the morning. This will save one of your guys a few hours making the rounds to all of them. Your fuel vendor will need a map of these locations also, so they won't run out of fuel.

The building department will also want to know where the towers are located, to ensure they aren't aimed at the neighboring homes.

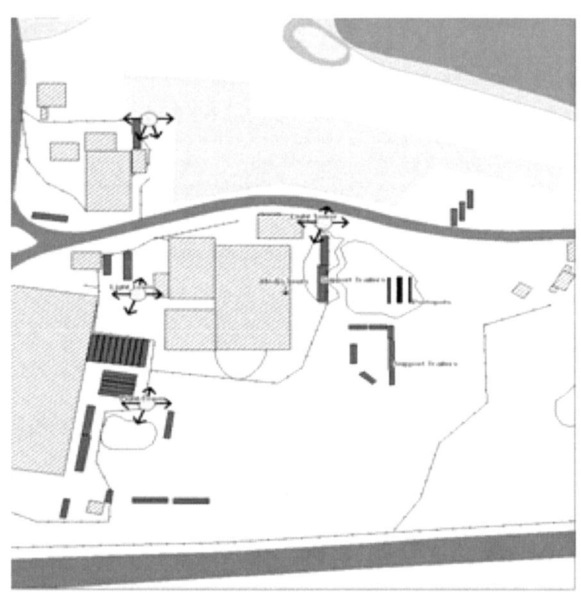

These are examples of typical light towers and their placement. The arrows indicate the direction the lights are aimed.

The building department will want to know the placement of the light towers on your site, to weigh the impact on the surrounding residences.

At some locations you might have the ability to tie your lighting equipment into existing shore power. This is preferable, if the cost is not too great or if you need power for an extended amount of time.

However, most power will be produced by portable generators of various sizes. Generators can be easily placed in most areas with a fork lift. When you are considering more than 80 generators, you need to know you can get them to the right areas. Larger generators, above 350KW, called twin packs, normally arrive and remain on a flatbed truck about fifty feet in length. It will often take some ingenuity and a good driver to get these units in place, as they don't arrive until the infrastructure has been built. The advantage of these units is that there is a backup generator on the same truck. It has an automatic transfer switch which maintains uninterrupted power. These units are normally 500KW and above, which means that fewer units will be required in a given area.

Photo provided by Aggreko

This is an example of a twin pack generator system. Two generators are housed: one primary and one backup. If the first one should fail for any reason, the power load transfers to the second generator by means of an automatic transfer switch.

Generators are not without problems; they require maintenance, depending on the number of days running and the length of time per day. They need fuel, so you better have additional fuel tanks provided for each set. It is imperative that the fuel vendor is dependable about showing up on time. If a generator runs out of diesel fuel, there is at least a 15-minute process to get it running again after receiving the fuel. Even with backup generators, it still takes time to transfer the cables from the primary to the backup.

When dealing with machines, things are bound to happen at the most inopportune time. Recently a main breaker on a 500 KVA generator (huge generator), burnt due to a fault in the cable. The breaker tripped like it was supposed to, but had to be replaced. Unfortunately, the tent which this generator was powering defaulted to emergency battery lights with over five hundred people inside. The electrical vendor had the breaker changed and the tent was back up and running within 25 minutes. This reinforces the need for experienced vendors who react well under pressure.

Scheduled maintenance usually takes place at night, when there is limited activity. When this maintenance is scheduled, you need to inform the people it will affect. Nightly cleaning crews can't clean the tents without power. Also, if you plan to switch areas from generator over to shore power, inform people who are using that power source that they will be down for the length of time required to make the switch. Failure to do so will cause hard feelings and lost work time.

A competent vendor knows all these things, and a good one will keep the down time to a minimum. It will be one of their goals during the event to keep all the generators working at peak efficiency.

When considering generators, remember the pricing should include placement of all units, freight to and from the site, standby personnel during peak times all event days, and associated maintenance costs. The standby generators should reflect less expensive pricing, as, after all, they are only a back-up, since the primary should never fail.

Each generator should be sound-attenuated, meaning you can stand next to one and carry on a conversation without shouting. Generators can run at 110% of capacity, but if it has to run that hard, someone miscalculated somewhere. Also make sure that the generators are surrounded by a fenced enclosure so spectators can't wander around them.

This will keep your building department officials happy.

Photo provided by Aggreko

This is an example of small generators that may be used during an event. These generators range from 60 KW to 250KW.

The HVAC vendor is responsible for providing the heating and air conditioning units. It is also their responsibility to determine the amount of air needed for each tent, based upon the size and the location of the event. The air conditioning units can be of different types, such as four-ton split units that can provide air conditioning and heat, or 20 to 50 ton units and chillers. Each has its own merits. The four-ton splits are ideal for the corporate tents, but they produce about five gallons in water condensation per hour, depending on weather conditions. Attention needs to given to where that water will run. You will need space between the tents for the condensers for each four ton unit.

The condensers may be stacked to help with space limitations.

The picture below shows the four-ton units on the floor before they are raised into position.

This illustration shows how the four ton air conditioning unit is incorporated into the décor.

The larger tents require bigger units that can throw the air further across the tent.

In addition, these units require more space outside the tent. Chillers are the most efficient but require even more space, not only for the air handlers but a place on level ground to park the trailer mounted units. However, they may be taken off the trailers if necessary. They can typically be placed 100 feet from the tent if required. Naturally, closer is better for the contractor.

Photo provided by Aggreko

This is an example of a chiller. The generator on the left is the power supply.

There is another air conditioner called a hush-pac. It is a 20 ton unit which is ducted through the tent wall. It has a supply duct and a return duct. These can be placed on raised scaffolding if the tent is above ground level. An example appears below.

It is sometimes necessary to supplement the clubhouse or locker room with air conditioning, but again, you need space outside the building for the air handlers and the power to run the units. You will also need windows through which the air duct is attached.

Even after all these things are considered and implemented, attention needs to be given to the expected temperature each day. If the temperature is going to be very hot, it may be necessary to maintain a cool temperature in the bigger tents

overnight to give them a head start.

Unfortunately, from time to time, the security guards in the tents find it too cold and turn up the temperature, and in some cases turn it off. If this is not noticed, by the time it is corrected, it may be too late and the air conditioners never recover. This means the tent would be warm in the middle of the day if the outside temperature is hot and there are a lot of people in the tent.

Other errors can occur as well. If a generator powering the four ton splits runs out of fuel and is restarted, the four ton units revert back to a default setting, and if unnoticed, it will have a problem catching up during the heat of the day. The normal default setting could have the temperature setting as high as 75 degrees. These are things which do happen and have happened. As a result, the electrical vendor should have nightly standby person to keep an eye on things.

The HVAC vendor will have additional units on hand, to switch out units that may be experiencing problems. However, if you have a site that is unusually tight, they may not be able to access the units. Think about these situations during the facility placement stage.

You will need to sit down with the director of corporate services to determine when generators and air conditioning units need to be available for the corporate villages. It is not uncommon to have generators running two weeks before the start of the event, to provide vendors the necessary power to complete their jobs.

These things need to be incorporated into the construction timeline so everyone is on the same page. When the event is over, it will be imperative that your electrical contractor disconnect the areas which need to be removed first, but make sure they also know what areas need to stay up and running.

This picture illustrates hush-pac air conditioning and how it is distributed through the tent wall. Grates are shown where the ducts come into the tent and are incorporated into the décor columns.

Photo provided by Aggreko

Chapter Twelve

ECOLOGY

There are a number of categories in this chapter, so we'll review them one at a time.

Portable toilets or portopots are a necessary part of any event. No one likes them, but everyone uses them. They should be strategically placed throughout the course with road access for heavy trucks to pump at night.

Make sure the vendor knows the routes to access each location. The drivers should be led by the hand to insure they know the route. I have pulled pump trucks out of the mud numerous times with a forklift because the drivers thought they knew the way. The portopots need to be placed around concessions or where quantities of people will see them, but out of sight from the television cameras. Single units at tee locations, inside the ropes, need to be placed for the players' use. The number of units will be determined by the size of the event but or a crowd of 40,000, the number of portopots ranges from 400 to 600 units, with an additional 17 to 20 disabled accessible units.

Photos provided by Mr. John

These are examples of a single portopot unit and a wheelchair accessible unit.

This being said, I have had some locations that I could have put two hundred units, but due to the configuration of the course, they all filled up prior to the end of the day. This was due to three fairways converging around this location and very high attendance. In these extreme cases, you will want to place a pump truck in the vicinity of a group of portopots if you have space to spare.

****

There will invariably be units off site at remote parking areas. The vendor needs to know where these are and how to access them. If he can't find them, he can't clean them which will make for a lot of unhappy spectators in the morning. Make sure your vendor knows that any units which will be seen by the public will be void of names or advertising if your venue has a policy prohibiting advertising. If he is using your event to purchase new equipment, this should not be a problem; advertising or stickers can be applied after the event.

You will need to order a number of units to accommodate vendors as they arrive on the premises. You also need to have portopots available around the merchandise tent if it opens early for a presale. After the event, don't forget to keep portopots on hand for your vendors when they break down the site.

It is advisable to create some kind of enclosure around the pods of units whether it is with lattice or chain link fence with windscreen attached. When the television cameras are panning the site, you don't want some poor guy coming out of a portopot zipping up.

With the vast quantities of portable toilets spread all over the course, you will need people to maintain the units, locking those which have seen too much use until they can be pumped out later. This maintenance crew is provided by the portopot company as part of the contract. Make sure that enough people are allocated for this job. You will need to provide these crews with golf carts, preferably, those with 4 foot flatbeds to haul supplies.

The health department will want to know what the plans are for hand wash stations at the portable toilet locations. While we are in favor of hand wash stations, the water runs out and can't be refilled until play is through for the day. This makes the problem worse than if you never had hand wash stations from the outset.

One solution is to provide sanitized towelettes or hand sanitizing liquid. It's not water, but it is sanitized and the health department sometimes agrees that it works for this particular situation. If you are lucky enough to have a permanent site, you can look into potable water and drain fields for hand wash stations.

The portopot company will need a relatively small compound to stage their big pump trucks. It does not have to be on site, but close is helpful. The vendor will also need an area on site to store basic supplies. The portopot company will find a place to dump the sewage, but you can save yourself some money and time if the health department will allow dumping into a sanitary manhole close to, if not on the site. Time is the main concern.

If a pump truck has to travel 30 minutes to dump the sewage and they have 600 toilets, assorted restroom trailers and holding tanks, well; you do the math. It will take a long time to finish even if they have a lot of trucks operating. Take into consideration that no restocking of any kind can begin before 8 or 9pm and the course has to be cleared by 6am.

Not a lot of time is it?

Make sure the crews have working radios. If you have a hot spot and can't get in touch with them, it will not be a pretty sight and someone will definitely remember it. It might behoove you to provide a cell phone after proper instruction on golf course etiquette.

All of the portable toilets should be the same color. If you are not dealing with a large company this could be impossible. If they all can't be the same color, try to make sure those on course are coordinated. The portopots at satellite locations do not need to be matching.

Sometimes the same company providing the portable units can also provide the restroom trailers. At approximately $6000 a piece for trailers make sure the specified locations make sense.

Typical trailer locations would include corporate villages, other corporate venues, media and merchandise tents, supplementing the clubhouse or members' tent, catering, and volunteer compounds. Typically 22 to 30 units are ordered depending upon the areas allocated. Not all the restroom trailers are financed by the event; some are paid directly by the vendors using them. Restroom trailers for an event of this magnitude are usually 35 feet in length and 15 feet wide when the stairs are extended. It will require some space to maneuver these units in place. In some locations it may be necessary to remove the stairs and build platforms between the units.

Knowing this in advance will help determine the flooring budget. Due to the weekly rental, it is usually not cost effective to contract the restroom trailers for more than the event duration itself. As a result, the trailers appear until a few days prior to the event which potentially places a strain on resources to get them in place, hook up power and water, and build the walk deck to each unit. The flooring vendor needs to know the schedule so they can be ready to spring into action. It will require the operations staff to be available to make sure that the units are delivered to the right areas.

No pressure.

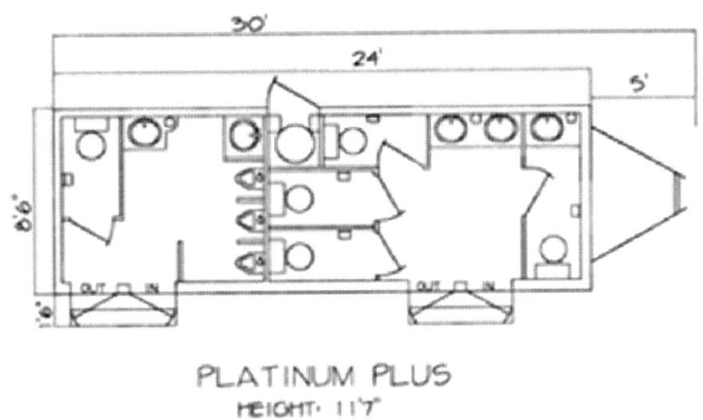

These are examples of a typical restroom trailer.

Photos provided by Mr. John.

If you have restroom trailers, it is essential to have restroom attendants to keep an eye on supplies and cleanliness of the units. If the units are sized correctly for each location, then operations run smoothly. However, if the units are overrun for Whatever reason, then the holding tank capacity can be reached quickly and the units have to be closed. This is a very bad thing because now it stresses out the other units which could also fill too quickly. In the potential problem areas, it is a good idea to park a pump truck close by to help alleviate the condition should it arise. There are no opportunities to bring a truck to a location on course during

play so it is imperative to have a back-up plan in place.

Make sure you include these personnel in the credential plan, for both on and off site workers.

Not many courses have potable water throughout the course. However, if there are water fountains on course it may possible to tap into this for water source depending upon the locations.

If the course doesn't have accessible water, then you will need to bring the water in. This won't be an inexpensive process. Typically, potable water for restroom trailers is needed, catering kitchen tents, some concession areas and any office trailer bathrooms. If the corporate tents requiring the restroom trailers are around the clubhouse, then you are fortunate as you can tap in to the water mains. These things should be considered during the site review.

Another source of water if water mains aren't close enough would be wells. As long as the health department doesn't have a problem, you can sink a well almost any place you need it, as long as there is a power source to run the pump. In some parts of the country it is allowable to use chlorinated water tanks which are gravity fed. You bring in the tank, chlorinate it, test it and off you go.

Whatever water source you use, be prepared to test the water supply prior, during and after the event. You will need to check with the health department as each locale has different regulations.

On course ecology amounts to a company providing people to make sure the course is devoid of trash throughout the day. If the site has a windy environment, this can be a challenge. The normal procedure is to break up the site into quadrants and assign groups of people to each.

It is their job to make sure their assigned area has no trash. Included in these quadrants are concessions, bleachers, office trailers, clubhouse exterior and offsite parking lots.

Work with the chosen company to determine the right amount of people per shift to get the job done. If you have too few people then they will never catch up and you run the risk of negative publicity. You will need to provide trash boxes or bags, which hang on a stand, and place throughout the course. Prime locations would be cross walks, concession areas, bleacher entries,outside-the-ropes on active fairways, around the clubhouse, parking lots, admission gates and generally anywhere spectators will be walking.

Over the years, I have had surprises in this area. For example, one year I worked with a civic group. During the planning process I had explained the vast scope of the job more than once, because I wanted to make sure they understood what was expected of them. The organization came back with a price which was accepted. During the latter part of the event, I received a call at 10:00 at night from the ecology crew leader telling me that he was pulling his crew unless he got more money. I asked him if he understood the scope that I explained to him and he said he had, but didn't think it was going to be this bad. I had to pay the extra money to get the job done, but made sure the powers above me knew what had transpired and to avoid using this group in the future.

The on-course ecology crew will need at least eight gas powered six foot flatbed golf carts to haul bags of garbage to the dumpsters throughout the course.

Provide them with radios and some of the supervisors with cell phones. You will tend to be everywhere throughout the venue, so when you see an area losing control you can report it immediately. Additional ecology is required for the smaller tents and office trailers. The occupants are instructed to leave the garbage outside the tents or trailers and the on course ecology team will pick it up before morning. Normally the caterer will handle their own garbage within their compound as they will have compactors and dumpsters. They will also remove the garbage from the major food tents and throw it into the dumpster provided. It is key that credentials affording proper access be given to this vendor.

If his people can't gain access, they are unable to clean and the dominoes start to fall. The schedule needs to be reviewed and the scope of work understood before an agreement can be signed. Surprises in this area will not be pleasant.

Corporate ecology is a different situation. This area is behind-the-scenes and the workers are responsible for hauling the bags of garbage placed outside the corporate tents to the dumpsters provided in each village. While this may seem easy, it is not. It is amazing how much garbage is generated by each corporate tent. Six foot flatbed golf carts will need to haul garbage to the dumpsters.

If the villages are hidden from play and spectators, it might be possible to use pick-up trucks to haul the garbage instead of golf carts. Either way, this is a never-ending task until the tents are clear. If you are unsure about the number of dumpsters necessary in the corporate villages or pavilion, talk to the caterer as they should know.

****

Another facet of corporate ecology is the nightly cleaning of tents. Each tent should be vacuumed and dusted. If you have 40 or 50 tents, that is a lot of square footage to cover especially if all the tents are not together. Cleaning supplies have to be moved to each village. This group will also provide people during the day to keep the common areas of the villages trash-free and will pitch in if there is a spill on the walk ways or public areas. Again, the credentialing process needs to be complete so the workers can gain access to their assigned areas.

Once the event is over, the ecology crew will stay on for three or four days to remove debris from the tents and the course. If there is anything left in the tents when they are disassembled, all of the contents will blow all over the course.

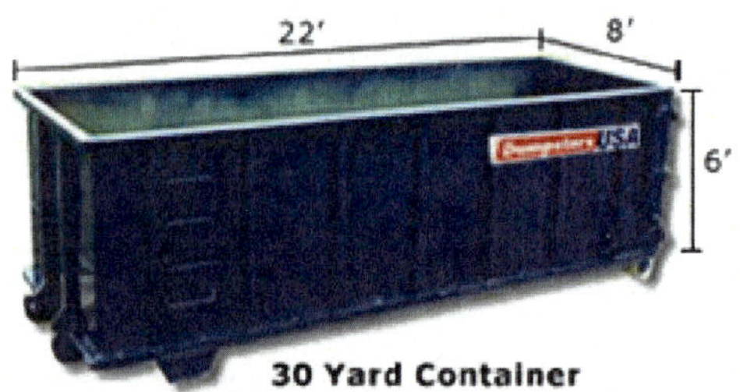

30 Yard Container

Even after the contracted ecology crew leaves, the operations staff will need to supervise temporary laborers periodically for weeks in order to insure all of the trash is picked up and thrown in dumpsters.

This is where we talk about dumpsters . . . the 30 yard capacity variety. The numbers will range anywhere from 29 to 41, depending upon the number of corporate tents, the size of the event and space limitations. There have been instances due to the lack of roads that standard pick-up trucks were located inside enclosures throughout the course then driven to a central point at the end of the day and the garbage thrown into a huge garbage truck.

It is preferable to place dumpsters around concession areas as they generate trash quickly, as well as areas which will generate tons of trash. Some examples would be the corporate areas, volunteer compound, parking areas and specified on course locations. By using the same method as used to determine where the ecology crews would work, the same thing for on-course dumpster locations.

Break the map into quadrants and place the dumpsters accordingly. The dumpsters need access by heavy trucks so roadways are necessary. Don't count on dry weather. If a heavy truck can't access the area because of wet conditions, don't put it there. There will be some sites where there are not many options. Work with the superintendent to find routes which would be acceptable.

Pre-determined routes need to be given to dumpster haulers and a walk-through is necessary to make sure the routes are understood. Don't forget that these workers are driving on course at night and there aren't many lights to guide them. Make it as easy as possible for them to perform their jobs.

All the dumpsters are in fenced enclosures with windscreen on the fence to hide them from view.In some vendor contracts, the vendor is responsible for the cost of dumpsters allocated to them after a specified number of pulls have been reached. Because of this, all dumpsters need to be labeled and the hauling company needs to maintain strict records. Each ticket needs to be signed by the vendor to insure they agree with the pull. This is great in theory, but very difficult to achieve. However, each vendor is responsible for signing their own dumpster tickets.

Once the event has ended, life becomes more frenetic for the dumpster hauler. Dumpsters are placed in every village so the décor company can tear out the decor overnight. The hauler will need two to three trucks assigned to hauling the corporate dumpsters as they are filled. They may pull each dumpster 3 or 4 times each day until all decor in the villages is gone. This will depend on the amount of décor in each village. You should have some kind of idea prior to the start of the event.

It is imperative the dumpster hauler understands the entire scope of their work. I had a case the dumpsters weren't pulled Saturday night as the landfill was closed on Sunday. We had planned for that, but the dumpster company only provided one truck driver on Monday who could not keep up. A quick email to the CEO of

the company and we had 8 trucks within the hour. After a few days of constant replacement we were able to scale back to a more normal schedule.

Be prepared to go to the top to get the job done. Your job may depend on it.

Before the event you will need to have dumpsters in the various operations areas. Catering, operations, bleachers, corporate villages need to be serviced during set-up. Dumpsters need to be where the workers are during set-up, otherwise they will have no place to throw the trash and your crew will be spending a lot of time picking up trash. Another way to help the vendors during set-up and tear-down is to place trash boxes in all areas where they are working.

The illustration shows trash box placements, denoted by the red x. If you are working with ecology groups who need a little direction and support, you can create maps such as this so there is no question where the trash boxes are to be placed on course or any other place. Armed with a map of the event, the ecology crew should be able to get the job done.

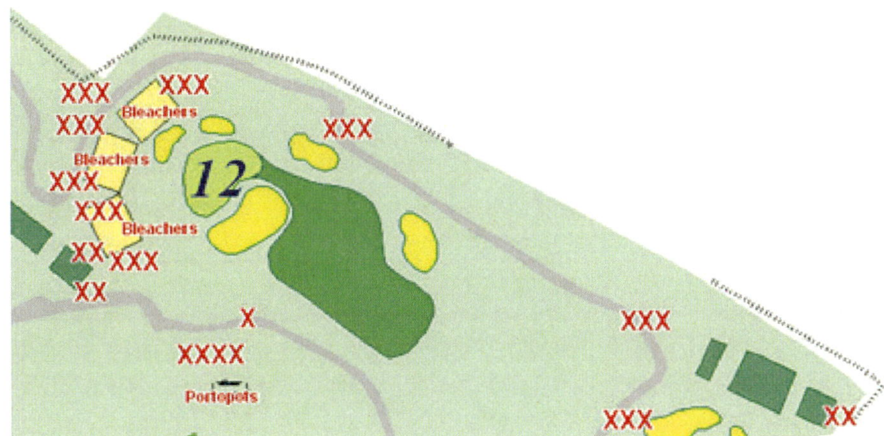

Chapter Thirteen

Communications

If things go wrong with communications, the whole world knows about it.

In today's world, communication represents many different things. Voice, Internet, wireless, voice over IP(VOIP), and many other private networks exist for television, on-course vendors (merchandise sales, gate scanning), or any other service that needs to be connected both on the course and to the outside world. Technology has continued to the point of being able to use a telephone service supported by the Internet, which requires less cabling. That's the upside. The downside is when the cable goes down, so do your phones.

Let's start with telephones. Once all facilities have been placed on the map, it will be evident where phones need to be located. To determine the number of hard phone lines needed in each area, you will have to draw upon past records or experience. Put together a spreadsheet divided by areas on a map, so the local communications companies can price the job accordingly. Under each area should be the name of the facility, number of lines, restricted or unrestricted, high speed and/or other needs. Include any off- site phone requests as soon as you are aware of them.

Once the local communications companies, as well as companies who specialize in special events, have looked at all areas, infrastructure or cable costs may be determined. This includes the cost to dig trenches and accommodate cable of sufficient size for each area. A separate price will be charged for each line ordered for the month's usage. All long distance charges will be separate depending upon the chosen carrier. This guide will serve as a gauge for phone costs.

Remembering that many voice lines are now able to exist on a data network, there will be different vendors who can provide better, more efficient solutions. Bandwidth is now replacing number of lines in many cases.

Once the number of phone lines has been established and areas designated, put together a scope of work and tie it into the map. Make sure you have planned additional lines in every area to accommodate ever- expanding requests. Between the Communications Company and input from other events, you should be able to gauge the number of extra lines needed. This is important because whoever is bidding on the project will need to know distances to accurately price the job.

Normally figure on four lines per corporate tent, knowing that some tents will only use two lines and others may need six. Enough cable needs to be available because if calculations are wrong, the week before the event is too late to pull additional cable.

New technology has allowed for the use of fiber optic cable to CAT 5 which have a large capacity for phone service. Include the television networks' needs at this time because the communications vendor will need to run cable to the network compound and it will be less expensive to do it one time. In addition, include any data requirements, fiber, as well as video circuits.

Call the television network contact to gather their specific information. They will be more than happy to provide this information as it assures them that service will be available. If you have the ability to provide a one point of contact for all communication needs ,you have just made your life easier by at least 100%.

Other things to include under the scope of work criteria are expectations about the features offered and at what price. Make sure to factor in labor of a normal work crew and the number of crews allocated to get the job done on time. Make the vendor aware that they are likely to be working Saturday and Sunday hours, not to mention holidays. The event will wait for no one, and they need to nderstand this fact from the outset. Bring up union issues and make sure laborers will be willing to cross a picket line, if necessary. Include the dry pair (dry pair refers to normal phone cable which runs from point A to B with a specific type of phone jack) for the scoring system as part of the estimate, if it is necessary at your event.

The communications vendor must be advised of the nature of the media operation and be prepared to fulfill orders on-site. It is not unusual for half of media attending the event to place orders on-site during the week of the event.

The good news is most of the media now rely heavily on cell phones. However their need for a large amount of bandwidth has replaced the phone line. It is common to need a large data connection to the internet to satisfy the photographers, writers and bloggers.

Media operations will be discussed in detail in chapter 22.

Include payphones in the scope of equipment needed, specifying potential locations and quantities. For large events plan to order around 100 pay phones. Attempt to locate the payphones where you already have phone facilities to make it easy. Hot spots for payphones will be the spectator bus loop, admission gates, Will Call, clubhouse, train station platform and concession areas. Inquire if the vendor will have a problem reaching the specified locations. Most, if not all events now use cellular technology and do not charge the spectators for its use, as it is very inexpensive.

Since new technology is being introduced all the time, you need to stay abreast of what is currently available. There are companies which will take the required communications from a demarcation location provided by the local phone company and distribute to all phones throughout the site. This company will coordinate all communication with the local phone company to accomplish what you have specified. They follow the same federal regulations as the phone company, but do this with wireless technology, fiber optics, and other hardware to make efficient use of the infrastructure. Instead of running oversized cable to each location, they transmit the required number of lines to each location using wireless technology, similar to what cellular companies use.

Oversize cable may handle 50 lines. With the new system, this size cable would not be needed as they would simply transmit additional lines to the new location as needed.

With the same technology, you could make the entire site a wireless network which would eliminate the need for cable modems and DSL line, however, a single large data connection is still necessary.

Wireless capability means less cable in the ground, which makes the superintendent happy about less trenching on his course. Less cable in the ground means less likelihood is less likely of being cut by mowers or fence posts being driven into the ground.

I'm not saying wireless technology is less expensive than the local phone companies, but it does add new benefits to the event. It provides more control over cabling costs and billing. The communications company is responsible for billing of the phones on-site which will free the accounting department from chasing charges by the local phone company. This will make accounting extremely happy.

It is interesting to see the innovations on the horizon. Once the specifications have been prepared you are ready to begin receiving bids. Know that not all phone companies are equal. There are some really good ones and there are extremely bad ones. You need to check the region to find out which companies do business there. If it is a known vendor, with a good reputation, your concern will be pricing. If it is a bad one, then you need to be concerned about everything.

In one situation, the phone company was so bad that we opted for new microwave technology. We investigated their past experience and found it to be the only viable option. It worked extremely well, except we lost a tower for some reason and the failsafe backup failed. What are the odds? The problem was found and fixed within a reasonable amount of time. It goes to show that even when you do everything right, something can and will go wrong.

At this point the vendor has been selected and they are working to get the cable installed to terminals in the areas on the map. The vendor will provide a block of phone numbers based on the quantities provided. From this block of numbers you can choose who has what number and you will need to decide whether the lines will be restricted or unrestricted. Unrestricted lines may call anywhere and incur long distance charges. Restricted lines are limited to local calls only. Needless to say, most lines are restricted. Make sure you pick easy numbers to remember for important areas.

The need exists for a switchboard and a main number which is published and available to the public. The switchboard will have 4 to 5 lines and operators to answer them. Ask your phone company about staffing the lines. Sometimes you can get volunteers, if they can attend the event in exchange for services. You should have an automatic attendant installed on the switchboard in the event that all the numbers are busy, with basic information such as tee times, volunteer information, ticket prices, and directions to parking areas.

A phone directory should be printed prior to the event. The hardest part of this process is to make sure you have the correct phone numbers listed in the directory. Try to spell all names correctly. In most cases, the phone directory may need to be reprinted due to additional names being added. You also may be able to have one of the sponsors absorb the printing costs.

Credentials for the phone company can be very numerous, due to the number of shifts required to cover the event. Provide on-site parking access for the phone trucks carrying the supplies. Everyone else can ride in these vehicles, or take the normal shuttle.

Unless there will be a herd of standby technicians, enough to cover each village, media, merchandise, the whole site, there will need to be golf carts allocated to communications crews. You will need to provide actual phone instruments at every location where there is a phone line. Usually, you can work out a deal with the phone company to provide the units with caveat that they are allowed to put a small advertising sticker on the underside of the handset where it can't be seen until you pick it up. You may also decide to purchase the phone sets and use them from year to year. The number of instruments could total over 700 depending upon the event.

There is also another sticker to be placed on the handset of all phones. It is the emergency number and it should be located on top of the handset, clearly visible.

In all probability, unless your scoring provider has wireless capabilities, you will have to run dry pair phones lines, or in some cases fiber optic cable to each area you want to have scoring information. Again, a dry pair is simply a standard phone

line cable running from point A to B. The scoring technicians will also need golf carts to get around the course to troubleshoot system problems. You will also need to determine where the scoring terminals need to be placed and how many per location. In this determination, don't forget television network's needs. As with all the other vendors, credentials and parking for the technicians will have to be addressed.

Let's discuss television feeds. The source for these feeds would either be the local cable company or Direct TV. First, determine the scope of work needed. This would include the numbers and locations of the televisions which have been assigned for the event. You can go back to your map to illustrate the locations and the vendors bidding on the job can determine their cable runs. If you are using the local cable company, try to coordinate the underground trenching work, so both cable and phone can go in the same trench. This will reduce your costs since both have to provide service to the same areas. The cable provider should be able to give you the cost per drop needed. There may also be a need for cable not on the course site, such as the day care facility. Make sure you include all potential needs and locations.

If you are providing high-speed internet access throughout the site, you will need to know the costs associated before offering the service to corporate clients.

Learn what channels each cable company has to offer. Hopefully, the networks televising the event will be among those carried. Normally the cable company has some spare channels not being used which might be available to broadcast special information about the event. If cable television can help spread the word about parking and traffic situations during the event, the cable company might be inclined to assist you.

In the scope of work, unions and the standby personnel needed during the event need to be addressed. The number of work crews necessary to complete the work on time will also need to be finalized. The parking situation on site during the event and the number of credentials will need to be settled as you don't need surprises at the last minute.

Repeat this same process with the satellite television company. The costs associated with this option should be less, as it requires less trenching and is less damaging to the ground. There could be some drawbacks however. You need to make sure that local channels can be received, and if they can't, determine if this is a problem for the corporate clients. If it is, normally you can use antennae to bring in the local signal where necessary.

Ask the marketing sales team. They will know the corporate clients' expectations. Make sure that the networks covering the event can be viewed on this system.

Beware of the unusual... in one instance, a contract had been awarded, yet the vendor backed out because he was unable to honor the quoted prices. If this occurs, you need to react quickly and call the competitor to ascertain interest. Hopefully, you can hold the original price and the event goes on. This example is provided because even when things should have been concluded, anything can happen.

It is your decision to pick the type of service desired, but there are other considerations to add to the mix and factor into the decision-making process. We'll discuss them in Chapter 14 under Corporate.

****

Let's discuss televisions. With the number of televisions required, align yourself with a manufacturer. The larger manufacturers are sometimes willing to barter the equipment needed for some kind of compensation which we will cover in Chapter 28, but let's discuss other particulars now.

The numbers and sizes of televisions and locations have been determined based on the facility placement map. There are other considerations: when and how the televisions are going to be delivered for starters. You will need to ask for a larger number than you actually need, because not all the televisions will work; some will arrive damaged or will become so before the event is over. Televisions are shipped to the site on tractor trailers of various lengths and it has to be understood that the trailers remain on site through the event.

This will require some site planning, as they will need to be staged in a place where your crew can access them without difficulty. When they are delivered is based upon how long it will take to distribute to all locations and the time it will take to test them.

A real simple test is needed. The television set is plugged into the power outlet and if the picture is clear and all the channels are present, then you are good to go.

Once distributed, security personnel need to be posted in the areas where televisions are situated to insure they won't be stolen.

A television distribution crew will need to be formed to deliver and install the televisions to the correct locations. The advent of flat screen televisions has reduced the number of back injuries incurred over the years, due to the weight of the larger sizes, but the crew will still need an assortment of equipment to install the televisions. They can use pick-up trucks in good weather but will need box trucks if the weather becomes a factor. Make sure the equipment remains in the boxes during transport and the trucks aren't moving at high speeds.

Televisions are sensitive to bumps and should be handled with care. Television distribution will also require two or three golf carts to service all of the areas quickly.They might need genie lifts to place some of the televisions into viewing cubes, which in some cases, are 9 to 10' off the floor.

During the event, this crew size is diminished, but is on hand in the event if televisions need to be replaced for whatever reason.

This is a vulnerable time as some tend to disappear during this period. Once taken to a central staging area, they are re-boxed and shipped to a local dealer for a sale. Generally you will circulate a price list of the televisions prior to the end of the event if it is part of the agreement to assist the television provider in selling the units, usually at drastically low prices. During the past few years, we have used a company to provide and install the televisions. It takes the stress off your crew and puts it into the hands of people who do this for a living: people who are good at it.

Immediately upon conclusion of the event, your crew immediately begins removing the televisions from the different areas. This is a vulnerable time as some tend to disappear during this period. Once taken to a central staging area, they are re-boxed and shipped to a local dealer for a sale. Generally you will circulate a price list of the televisions prior to the end of the event if it is part of the agreement to assist the television provider in selling the units, usually at drastically low prices. During the past few years we have used a company to provide and install the televisions. It takes the stress off your crew and puts it into the hands of people who do this for a living; people who are good at it

Cell phones have become more of a norm at events and this is a mixed blessing. There are so many used by spectators that it has become difficult to maintain a semblance of silence during events.

Everyone thinks they need their phone, and steps will need to be taken to make sure unauthorized cell phones do not sneak their way in and cause a disruption. Normally, these phones, as well as other items, are found during the pat down process at the admission areas.

Many events do allow cell phones. It permits the spectators to take pictures of the players on days specified and, on occasion, provides applications for assistance in getting around the course. There are a wide variety of phone applications; some provide streaming video of play, while others just provide the facilities' locations and my personal favorite: where you parked your car.

Some of the support staff at the event will need cell phones to communicate quickly and add ten to it, as there will be people who were forgotten somewhere along the way. During this process remember the key vendors, those you will need to talk to quickly and privately concerning a number of issues. Determine the number you need and then potential problem areas which might occur such as the fuel truck is late, or the air conditioner at tent number twelve is about to stop.

Take delivery of some phones for the vendors early and then phase in the rest of the phones prior to the event.

Some manufacturers have a radio feature built into the phone itself which comes in handy. This feature can reduce the number of walkie talkie radios needed.

Your provider has the ability to input some of the commonly used phone numbers of key vendors on the phones provided.

Whoever provides the cell phones will need to have technicians on site during the event to work out any problems and to deal with dead batteries. These responsibilities will be addressed in the vendor agreement.

Another solution is to purchase inexpensive cell phones which are enough to cover your needs and pay for coverage for the period needed. As the phones break or get lost,you can easily replace them. If the coverage on your site is bad now, it would be advantageous to have this additional coverage activated as soon as possible. At the very least, it should be operational when your major vendors begin set-up.

On-site parking will need to be provided for a few technicians with tools, others may access the normal shuttle system. Credentials are very important for the technicians, in the event the cell site goes down and they have to react quickly. A cart will need to be provided or someone made available to take them where they need to go.

Because there is the potential of so many cell phones being on site, either the ones you have provided or permitted, it is a good idea to have some kind of sticker system for authorized phones to allow security to weed out the unauthorized phones which should not get through the admission gate. What will happens to the cell phones security catches trying to get through the admission gates? Stay tuned for the answer in the next chapter. On one radio there can be a number of active channels. Some radios have six channels, others much higher; the size of your event will dictate the number of channels per radio. Not every group needs to talk to each other which can reduce the number of channels needed on each radio. However, you will need to be able to talk to every group, so there will be a handful of radios with that capability.

Please note that every group needs access to the medical channel in the event of an emergency situation. Normally there will be a Joint Operations Center where each safety agency will set up to monitor all emergency transmissions. This will be discussed in greater detail in the next chapter.

It takes a great deal of thought to determine each grouping. You don't want too many different vendors on the same channel, as some will over power the others with constant communications. It must be conveyed that radios are not telephones and that ALL communication needs to be concise and to the point. Nothing is more aggravating than a person rambling on about something when people are waiting to communicate. Once you have the groupings and numbers of radios per group worked out, create a grid on a spreadsheet. This will help you review the numbers before choosing radio vendors.

Nothing is more aggravating than a person rambling on about something when people are waiting to communicate. Once you have the groupings and numbers of radios per group worked out, create a grid on a spreadsheet. This will help you review the numbers before choosing radio vendors.

Create a scope of work for the bid process which would include site visits by the vendor to determine the coverage area, cost of repeaters(towers which boost the signal for longer distances), cost per rental radio, cost for lost radios, as well as ear phones and microphones. Included in the bid should be standby personnel to be on site during the event.

Make sure the vendor understands that you want no hidden costs associated with the event.

There may be a need to have some radios available prior to the start of the event for operations staff and vendors to use, if cell phones are not available. You may also choose to keep some radios after the event for the same purpose during tear down. Make sure all these things have been thought through while preparing a contract.

Once the radio vendor has been chosen, you can fine tune the numbers and groupings. The vendor may make suggestions from time to time based upon their experience at other events. The numbers can become staggering, if not kept in check.

Use common sense.

Chapter Fourteen

Security and Law Enforcement

There are usually two types of security, contract and law enforcement. Both are very necessary and both tend to get expensive. With the experience of 9/11 security has taken a whole new meaning. This chapter will not discuss the actual security measures, but rather the process you need to get the information. Contract security is hired to provide service in a number of areas: secure the corporate tents from overnight theft, provide roaming guards at night on course, check credentials and disallowed items at admission gates, and check credential access at the sensitive areas. It is a big job and the number of hours required is tremendous.

Begin by listing all the areas where coverage is needed. It might be helpful to put this on a spreadsheet. Once the locations are picked, break the areas up into shifts of 8 to 12 hours each. If you choose 12 hour shifts, then you will be paying overtime but will require fewer guards.

One benefit of longer shifts is that the guards begin to recognize the people coming into their area, but unless they are given breaks on a timely basis you will begin to lose guards. Let's keep this based on 8 hour shifts: normal shifts would be 6am to 2pm, 2pm to 10pm and 10pm to 6am. Put down the number of guards per location and write a job description of what you expect these guards to do.

The security company will be obligated to run background checks on all the employees hired for the event. This will help to insure the safety of the players and spectators. The guards will experience the same pat-down process for disallowed items as the spectators before they are allowed on the site.

A different set of criteria exists for the guards used prior to the event and after the event is over. Prior to the event the main purpose of the guards is to deter the theft of items in the corporate villages and to prevent damage to the event site. Following the event the same criteria should be maintained. It takes a great deal of thought to determine each grouping. You don't want too many different vendors on the same channel, as some will over power the others with constant communications. It must be conveyed that radios are not telephones and that ALL communication needs to be concise and to the point.

Another solution is to purchase inexpensive cell phones, which are enough to cover your needs and pay for coverage for the period needed. As the phones break or get lost, you can easily replace them. Depending upon where the event is located, you may need to have the cell phone provider bring in temporary cell sites, called COWS, to boost the coverage in the immediate vicinity of the event. A site survey should be conducted to determine the normal coverage and then, projected attendance considered to determine if additional coverage is needed.

If a temporary cell site is needed, find out the requirements from the cell provider, especially the size, location, power requirements, projected height and most importantly, when it will be operational. We have had locations where all of the major cell phone providers wanted to be on site. It took a lot of space to accommodate all of their requirements.

The guards at the admission gates are checking credentials and tickets and are on the look-out for disallowed items. Most of these items will be picked up during the pat-down process. Every person entering the grounds will be patted down or have a magnetic wand passed around their body to identify items not allowed on site.

Disallowed items will have been publicized and are specified o[illegible]s so it should be no surprise to spectators when they arrive at the eve[illegible]

The items listed below are a good representation of items not allowed on shuttle buses or through admission gates:

- **Blackberries, PDA's or any other type of portable email device**
- **Noise-producing and/or electronic devices (including MP3 Players)**
- **Bags larger than 8"wide x 8"high x 8" deep in its natural state, this size may vary per event.**
- **Cameras and camcorders (permitted for Practice Rounds only_**
- **Cases and/or Covers (such as chair or umbrella sheath)**
- **Televisions and/or radios, unless provided and permitted by tournament officials**
- **Containers and/or coolers**
- **Food and/or beverages**
- **Ladders and/or step stools or other similar items**
- **Bicycles**
- **Lawn and/or folding armchairs**
- **Metal-spiked golf shoes**
- **Pets (other than service animals)**
- **Signs, posters and/or banners**
- **Weapons (regardless of concealed weapon permit, including but not limited to firearms to knives).**
  - » **Armed off-duty Peace Officers are the exception to the "no-firearms" rule.**
  - » **Armed off-duty peace officers will be issued a distinguishable object such as a pin**
- **Any other items deemed unlawful or dangerous by tournament officials and / or event security personnel, in their sole discretion**
- **All persons subject to a reasonable search**

Unfortunately people tend to do what they want regardless of what is expected. If items are found, two things could transpire. Either the person is denied access to the grounds unless the offending article is removed, or the person can check the item for a fee at the disallowed item trailer. Some of the vendors or staff will need to enter the site with some of the disallowed items but a special tag should have been created for these instances.

It is the security contractor's responsibility to insure that their guards have adequate breaks and water since they need to remain at their posts for long periods of time.

In selecting a contractor, check references carefully, talk to the other venues to make sure that they have the necessary experience. Again, the least expensive contractor may not be the best for you. Find out what percentage of guards for your event will be temporary hires or existing staff. Will there be strong supervision and how many supervisors per number of guards?

The contractor should be picked far enough in advance of the event to allow them to hire quality personnel and to conduct event specific training sessions. Each training session should include slides, pictures or diagrams of each post, if available, to familiarize the guards about what to expect. They should be instructed on when and where they are to take breaks, have lunch, how to dress, and other details.

Guards should be given explicit instructions on golf course etiquette. This means Don't drive golf carts on the greens and tees! I cannot tell you how many times I

have chased guards in carts off greens or had to apologize to a superintendent for errant behavior by a non-uniformed security employee.

It should NEVER happen.

Work out the method that the guards will use to access the site for the first shift in the morning. They have to arrive early enough to be checked in, patted down and on post at the assigned time. If the security personnel are accessing your shuttle system, assure them that the buses will be there at the proper time to get them to work. If this system breaks down, you have no guards on your first shift.

During the event it is very common to notice areas where assigned guards aren't needed and other locations where they are. Generally, it is not a problem to shift guards to other locations, but if you need additional guards, it could become problematic until the following day. If the company is large enough and you have done your homework the addition of a few guards will not be a problem. However, adding 5-10 guards could potentially be a problem due to lack of proper training of the new guards. Make sure to thoroughly review the site so the number of guards is closely calculated.

The contract should specify the guards will be responsible for turning on the light towers at dusk in their areas and turning them off in the morning. It would also help if they would monitor the fuel levels.

In addition to posted guards at specified locations, you may opt to use wireless cameras in areas prone to theft, such as the interior of corporate tents, or corporate merchandise storage units. These cameras may be set-up with motion detectors so they only record when motion is detected. Cameras never fall asleep. The wireless feature allows the cameras to be view from a specific web page on the internet. You may never need this kind of security, but be aware of its availability.

After the facilities have been placed on the map and the parking areas have been determined, law enforcement officials need to be contacted to discuss routing of shuttles, traffic patterns to the parking lots, on-site spectator movement, and player needs.

A lead agency needs to be determined whether it is the State, County or local authorities.

The primary responsibilities of law enforcement include the following:

- Player Compound - Law enforcement officers will guard the player secure areas, including player parking, player hospitality, locker room, practice range and putting green.

- Player Pathways through Mass Spectator Areas - Should it be determined that marshals cannot handle a given situation directly involving players, then law enforcement will be added to that location...examples would be exit to 18 green, entrance to 1 Tee, 10th Tee shuttle, media flash and walkways to and from player parking areas.

- Player Escorts - At minimum 12 officers are normally assigned to escort top-tier players during their rounds. These law enforcement officers should be a visible uniformed deterrent and are needed to clear walkways, address hecklers, and work with players as balls leave the ropes.

- General Public Screening Areas - At any screening location the general public gets checked for disallowed items, a law enforcement officer will be available to provide support for private security and handle unusual situations. The officer will have the final word when dealing with anyone trying to bring in a firearm.

- Major Spectator Gathering Areas - An officer will be assigned to any area spectators gather in masses and where movement might become difficult in cases of emergency. Examples would include the merchandise tent, the Trophy Club, 18 green and other congested areas.

Sector Response Teams on the golf Course - The golf course has been divided into reasonable sectors and law enforcement officers assigned to each sector. These law enforcement teams should be able to react in a timely manner to situations such as player heckling, disorderly spectators, player evacuation procedures, and crowd control issues.

A Joint Operations Center (JOC) will be created to house all emergency services under one roof for easy communication between agencies. These agencies would include Communications, Medical, Fire Services, Law Enforcement, Private Security and Tournament liaison.

Package Plan and Procedures

Unattended packages are those that have been left behind by someone. An unattended package does not pose a risk to anyone, but it needs to be cleared by a law enforcement official. If the package poses a risk or threat it is referred to as a Suspicious Package

Suspicious Package

The suspicious package must be cleared or removed by either ATF, FBI or a designated Bomb Technician.

In the event of a bomb threat, the individual receiving the call should gather as much information as possible to assess the validity of the threat. A threat assessment will be done in coordination with the Joint Operations Center (JOC)

At a minimum,

- All law enforcement, security personnel and volunteers will be notified of the threat. Each
officer and volunteer will inspect the area they are assigned for any suspicious packages.

- If a suspicious package is found, the Joint Operations Center (JOC) will be notified immediately. The command staff assigned to the JOC will coordinate the appropriate incident response "Do not touch or move a suspicious package or device"

- Any decision to evacuate the area will be made in coordination with the JOC and tournament officials

- Officers will assist with the orderly evacuation and insure everyone in the affected area has been evacuated

- Officers will remain at their posts until they receive instructions to evacuate by the JOC. Once advised to evacuate, officers will expand the exterior evacuation perimeter to ensure safety of all persons at the event.

- The evacuation will remain in effect until the JOC gives the order to resume normal operations in and around the affect area

A great deal of energy goes into safe guarding everyone at the event. Every truck entering the property at night will have credentials checked and the truck will be swept by a bomb-sniffing dog. The clubhouse and other facilities frequented by players will also be swept.

We all need to be aware of the times we are living in and take measures to insure the safety of those attending the event.

The green, numbered dots represent the security locations in this area. The next page is a database which would refer to the numbered positions.

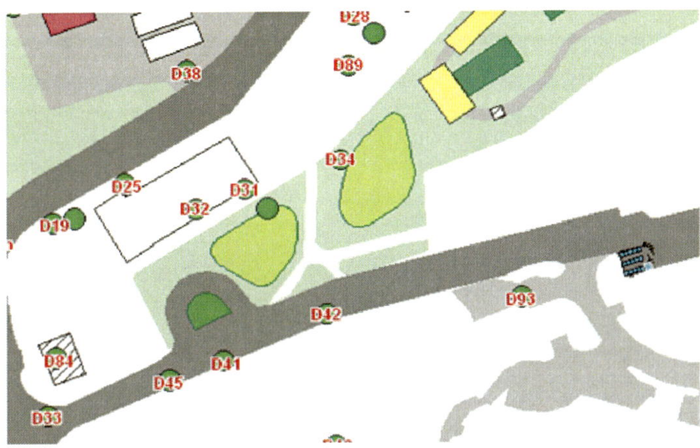

Open air events are the most difficult to secure, as there are normally acres of open space protected by a fence at best. These venues require more resources to protect than a contained event, like a stadium or arena.

Security Posts

Number	Location	Date	Time	Hours	Days	People	Total
D26	Townhouse Admissions-Car Passes	June 12- June 18	6am-8pm	14	7	1	98
D27	Townhouse Admissions-Car Passes	June 12- June 18	6am-8pm	14	7	1	98
D28	Golf Shop-Security-Theft	June 12- June 18	7am-10pm	15	7	1	105
D29	Golf Shop-Security-Theft	June 12- June 18	7am-10pm	15	7	1	105
D30	Golf Shop-Security-Theft	June 12- June 18	7am-10pm	15	7	1	105
D31	US Open Store-Security-Theft	June 12- June 18	6am-10pm	16	7	1	112
D32	US Open Store-Security-Theft	June 12- June 18	6am-10pm	16	7	1	112
D33	Iron Gate-Car Passes	June 12- June 18	6am-10pm	16	7	1	112
D34	Putting Green- Crowd Control	June 12- June 18	6am-6pm	12	7	1	84
D35	Putting Green-Crowd Control	June 12- June 18	6am-6pm	12	7	1	84
D36	Post Office Lot- Car Passes	June 12- June 18	6am-7pm	13	7	1	91
D37	Post Office Lot-Car Passes	June 12- June 18	6am-7pm	13	7	1	91

This grid illustrates a security database created within the mapping program. Once completed, it may be given to the various security companies along with the map depicting the locations for bid purposes.

Chapter Fifteen

PARKING AND TRAFFIC

Parking areas are without a doubt one of the most important concerns for any event regardless of magnitude. The size of the lots is determined by the number of cars coming to the event which is based on the attendance. Not all the spectators will be parking in the same lot. Special groups need their own lots such as volunteers or corporate hospitality patrons.

Special lots may need to be in a preferential location closer to the site than the general lots. Some groups may need to park on site. Depending upon the location of your event, the availability of close parking lots may not be feasible and in such a case, a shuttle system may need to be implemented.

For a shuttle system, the best case would to find suitable lots within twenty minutes travel time from your site. Upon occasion, this will not be the case. If the travel time is going to be substantially more than twenty minutes then the media department may need to assist in getting the word out.

Not every shuttle plan is perfect, and you can only deal with the cards you are dealt. People coming to the event will need to be informed of the plan. It will also need to be explained that it is the best plan available and not adhering to it will cause longer waiting times and traffic.

Most people will arrive between the hours of 7:00 and 9:00 am, so be ready.

Parking lot surfaces can vary drastically. The optimum surface is always asphalt as it is unaffected by wet weather. The same holds true for crushed rock surfaces, but dust will be a concern due to the amount of traffic in the lot. There are a few really good products which can be used to minimize the dust but research them carefully, not all of them work.

The least desirable and the most common would be a grass surface. Grass is fine during dry conditions, but during wet conditions, it could become a nightmare. Cars getting stuck in the mud necessitates tow trucks to pull them out. The day after rain, these lots may be unusable. If it is the plan to park on grass surfaces, there needs to be a back-up parking plan in the event of bad weather.

Sometimes there are temporary crushed gravel roads placed in grass lots to assist the cars during wet weather. If cars can reach the temporary road, then they are assured of leaving the lot. If 10,000 people are expected, find a lot large enough to accommodate 5,000 cars or 40 acres.

The typical formula is two people per car, in order to size the lots and calculate the number of cars for each lot. It equates to around 125 cars per acre. A great deal will depend upon who is assigned to the parking lot to assist with the parking of the cars. Don't forget, as cars leave during the day, the open spots in the lot can be filled with incoming cars.

An example of a typical parking lot is illustrated below.

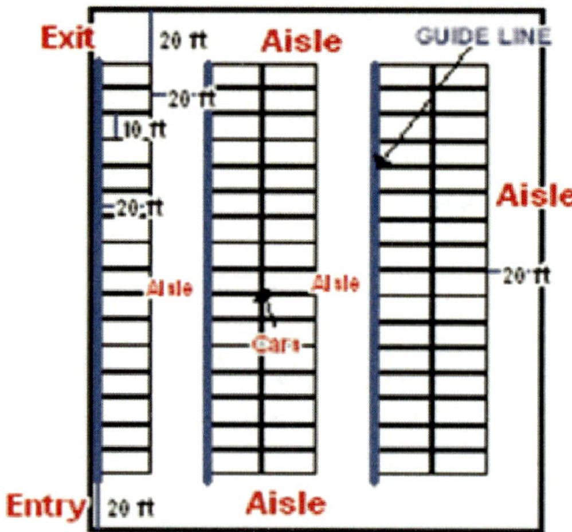

It is always helpful to have more than one access point into the lot to get the cars off the road quickly. It a perfect world there would be a stacking area for cars off the roadside as they enter the lot to keep the normal traffic moving. There need to be lines painted (make sure the paint is bio-degradable) on the surface which will act as a guide where to park the first row of cars.

A standard dimension for a parking space is 10'x 20'.

You may be able to squeeze the cars a little tighter, but I don't advise going too much smaller as the doors will be hitting adjacent cars. Leave at least 20 feet for access roads before you start the next guide line. This process will continue throughout the lot. There need to be signs with large letters identifying the aisles to assist the spectators finding their cars at the end of the day.

Unless the event is very small it is advisable to contract with a parking company. If this is the case, identify this vendor early as they can be a wealth of knowledge. The parking company can assist in developing the numbers of cars per lot as well as the number of parking attendants necessary in each lot to get the cars parked quickly and uniformly. This is a large undertaking and you need to be assured that the company you are using has the experience to make this a seamless operation. In addition to the parking attendants, there needs to be a supervisor in each lot to handle any parking-related problems which may arise.

The parking company will also assist in laying out the shuttle bus queuing area. This is an extremely important function. There needs to be order in loading the buses coming to and leaving the event. The vendor will create a queuing maze which the spectators enter, winding back and forth until they reach the front of the line where the buses are staged. The attendants will line the people up in chutes in numbers which will fill one bus. When the buses arrive, they line up in front of the chutes and all the buses are loaded simultaneously. The size of the event will dictate how many buses should be loaded at one time at the end of the day.

It is optimum to load at least eight to ten buses at a time.

It is normally not a problem in the morning getting the spectators to the event on the shuttle buses as they are constantly in motion and spectators tend to trickle in, but at the end of the day, there may be large crowds waiting to leave and the buses need to be waiting.

This is also true in the event of rain or potential rain. The buses need to be in queue waiting to load as a potential storm approaches. The number of buses in the shuttle system is proportional to the distance they have to travel and return, as well as traffic conditions.

The object is never to have a lack of buses loading. If spectators see that the lines aren't moving or there are no buses in the pick-up area, then they tend to get irritable. The shuttle system is the first thing they see in the morning and the last thing they see at night and if it isn't working, they might not follow the plan and really cause traffic problems. To determine the number of buses you will need, you first need to know the capacity of the buses and then the time it will take for the one bus to make a round trip from the site to the parking area and back. For instance, if it takes a bus one hour to make a round trip including loading and unloading and a bus holds 47 people, you can move 47 people per hour with one bus.

Theoretically, if you can load and unload 60 buses in one hour, you will be moving 2,820 people per hour (47 people per bus x 60 buses). If the parking lot is close and you can make two trips per hour, you will double the amount of people you can move to 5, 640. Naturally, if you can load more buses on site at one time, you can move more people.

This scenario will also be affected by the cost per bus, traffic conditions, and the actual time it takes to load a bus, reach the parking lot and return. Other factors play into the equation. For example, if big name players will finish play by 1 pm., then you might see a mass exit to the buses for the parking lots. People typically begin leaving an event around 3:30 pm and the biggest surge occurs between 6pm and 7:30 pm.

No one wants to be stuck in line waiting for a bus so some will leave earlier and others later, but the buses tend to move the crowds to the parking lots quickly if you have planned correctly.

The parking company is in constant communications with the bus dispatcher to determine the location and status of the buses at all times. They should have the ability to add or reroute buses depending upon the ever-changing situations.

Recently this axiom was not followed and too many buses were allocated for spectators after Tiger finished his round, but no one left the site. They stayed for the finish of Phil Mickleson's round.

This created a need for more buses to move the spectators at the end of the day than were allocated, but there were no additional buses to draw from due to misallocation of the resources available and not enough money in the budget to compensate.

Calls were made to every possible bus company in the area to try to get back on track. This caused the budget to be thrown out the door as the only priority was to get the spectators home. This emphasizes the fact that even when the best minds in the transportation business get together to project what should happen, it doesn't always follow the plan.

There should have been a larger budget to allow more buses to be available to accommodate the ever-changing situation

The situation created a waiting time of two hours until we were able to restore the number of buses needed.

Once the situation was recognized it was too late to find an expedited solution.

Buses are usually broken down (no pun intended) into two types; school buses and coach buses. If there is a relatively long distance to cover before reaching the site, coach buses may be used. They are more comfortable and have air conditioning, but are generally more expensive. If it is a short run, school buses may be used. Although the space is a little tight in the seats and they have no air conditioning, most people don't complain because the ride is not long. When considering the shuttle buses, spend some time working through the number of buses needed for your event. The buses should enter the lots from a different route than the cars so as not to be caught up in the traffic. This is always the optimum plan, but if this is not the case, it may require more buses to compensate. Where the buses will be staged when not in use, as well as at night when the event is over, need to be worked out.

The bus drivers will need a break area and at some locations you may be asked to assist with housing for the drivers. Generally, the bus drivers stay close to the site due to the number of hours they are working. The cost of housing will be added to the cost per bus, so it is better for you to find the housing as you might be able to work a deal with a nearby college or apartment complex. Sometimes the cost of food for the drivers is included in the contract. These things will need to be worked out with the bus companies.

Fueling will be a consideration as there are a lot of buses needing fuel and a normal gas station just isn't going to cut it. A tanker truck or two may be needed to satisfy this requirement.

Bus drivers' schedule will be established. Bus drivers can only work so many hours per day so make sure you have enough personnel to cover the late shift. There may be additional needs for buses during the event and you have to research all these things so they don't slip through the cracks. For example, the player's wives may need to be transported or VIP's picked up at a golf course down the road. Carefully calculate the cost per hour per bus, based on the schedules and the number of buses to make sure your budget is large enough for your needs.

Regardless of the bus type, there needs to be a drop-off point for each shuttle close to, if not on, the event site. If there isn't an area large enough to accommodate at least 8 to 10 buses to be staged on a hard surface, a temporary road needs to be constructed to accommodate the drop-off and pick-up process.

In a previous chapter temporary roads were discussed, but to re-emphasize, with the amount and frequency of large heavy buses running on a temporary crushed rock surface all day, the road will break down eventually, unless the sub base of the road is hard. Be prepared for this occurrence with equipment or heavy duty traffic plates to repair the damage.

It may be necessary to hold up the bus movement to achieve this, but normally between the parking company and event operations, a favorable time for the repair will be figured out. If heavy duty mats are used, as discussed in the construction chapter, you will not need to worry about the temporary road as the mats can withstand substantial abuse associated with the weight and number of buses. Shuttles from other lots also need a drop-off location in close proximity to the event site. Some walking may be necessary to reach the site once dropped off by the shuttle. The number of lots and shuttles will determine the number of drop-off sites needed.

Other suggested modes of transportation might include a train if the station is

close enough to the site. Reducing the size of the lots needed due to people taking other modes of transportation can help reduce the burden on the shuttle system. Check with the neighboring towns to see if they are planning to run shuttles from the town to the site. This would definitely impact the system you already have in place. There may not be room to accommodate another shuttle drop on your site. It is better to find this out sooner, rather than later, so the situation may be dealt with.

The same holds true for hotel shuttles. Hotels may think this would be a wonderful service to provide to guests, and it would, provided there is room for yet another shuttle drop on site. Naturally, if there is room and traffic flow can be controlled, you might want to consider additional shuttles to help reduce the traffic to your lots.

There have been situations when the club has struck a deal with the local municipality to provide buses for shuttles to be involved with the event. During one particular event, the buses showed up late or not at all and I had to scramble to locate more buses quickly. Due to the additional waiting time for buses, people were becoming restless and I had to shift police to the bus loop for crowd control.

A situation like this could create unrest on-site caused by impatient spectators waiting for the buses to arrive. This would have been compounded had it been raining.

If there is a rail system close to the site, you may be able to talk to the operators about adding more trains for the event. If the number of people attending is high enough, then the railroad will certainly see the benefits from running more trains. Schedules may need to be adjusted during the time of the event, fares modified once additional train cars are staged on adjacent tracks to accommodate the demand. However, if it is cost effective and the facilities are available, this will be a good alternative.

There will need to be an area set aside at the train station for people to queue so they can purchase train tickets before loading the train from the platform. They will need to be controlled and lined up in an orderly fashion on the platform to get on the train quickly when it arrives. The flow will be normally heavy on the inbound between 7 am to 11:30 am and outbound from 3:30 pm to 7:30 pm.

To maximize the usage of the rail system to your event, the railroad may offer promotions or a newly printed schedule for riding the train. The media department can assist by getting the word out and encouraging spectators to ride the train. If it is a good experience then more people will take advantage of not being stuck on congested roads. Parking passes allowing the ability to park on-site will be worth their weight in gold. Because the site normally has limited parking, special attention needs to be given to the number of passes necessary per category. Some of the usual categories are player, media, VIP, all access, night access only and vendor.

Every special lot, whether it is on-site or not, will need a parking pass. The general public parking lots usually do not require parking passes unless the lots have limited capacity. If there are have lots of limited capacity with no specific parking passes, there is a chance that one lot will be full and the other lot way underutilized.

Special lots requiring such passes might include volunteers, media, corporate, staff, VIPs and members. There are a limited number of all area access passes printed for the operations trucks and parking crews, which need to drive to all parts of the site, as well as the vendors who have enough room in their compounds

to park. There will be other vendors who will need to park on site with trucks having backup supplies.

It would behoove you to carve out a space onsite to act as a backup contingency area in the event that you need more parking. With increased security, you will need to provide access passes to service vendors who will be accessing the property at night. All trucks entering the site will be swept by the police, so make sure these passes are distributed.

It will be advantageous to produce a grid showing each lot, number of cars, parking pass, type of shuttle, the times the shuttle runs and the time it takes to get from the lot to event drop off. This task should not be treated lightly. An error here could cause gridlock around the drop off area as well as overflowing lots.

At some events it may be necessary to have a traffic engineer review the proposed traffic patterns and car counts for the suggested routes to the parking lots. Make sure the engineer understands the parking and shuttle objectives. Solely basing traffic flow on the numbers of cars on the road systems may completely disrupt the spectator movement on site. These components need to coexist in harmony.

Drive the traffic routes yourself to better understand the traffic movement. Explore other routes for alternative traffic flow. You may find a better route than the one being proposed, but know that the locals usually know the peak traffic periods and the areas which receive the most congestion.

This is an example of a variable message board.

Once the traffic plan has been drafted, the law enforcement agencies will need to review the plan in order to assign various traffic and officers positions. When this is done, they can assign traffic cops at the necessary locations for traffic control. A traffic cone plan needs to be devised to allow easily identifiable lanes which the public will understand.

If barricades are to be used at certain intersections, the time of placement and removal needs to be decided and communicated to the public through the media. In some cases the cones and barricades stay up for the entire event; in others they are removed at night and redistributed in the early morning.

The Department of Transportation, (DOT), will often help to provide most of the necessary cones and barricades necessary for traffic control. Upon occasion it may be necessary to install temporary stop lights to ease the burden on an officer standing in the middle of the road directing traffic. As a rule no officer enjoys standing in the middle of the road as it leaves them vulnerable to being hit by a car.

The DOT may also provide variable message boards where necessary, as they are large and can be seen easily. I have also used this type of sign during pre-tournament times to inform the public of construction traffic in the area and to advise to slow down.

Electronic message boards may also be used to inform truckers, delivering material, where to stage the trucks until you are ready to place them. This will save time when trying to track down the large quantities of trucks which come to the site on a daily basis during setup. If the traffic plan is sound and people adhere to the plan, then in all probability, things should go well. Traffic accidents which occur in the area of the site would tend to cause major tie-ups on a normal day. The volume of cars coming to and leaving your event just makes the situation much worse.

Tow trucks are on hand for this contingency and the police are always on the look-out; quickly clearing the roadway of the obstruction, to keep traffic moving. It's a beautiful thing.

Remember to contact the state, county or local agencies who control unrelated road construction in your area to make sure that the construction will be completed by the time the event starts or at the very least, postponed or stopped during the event time period. If notice is given far enough in advance, they will generally cooperate, especially if they understand that there will be additional congestion created as well as the positive economic impact the event may have on the surrounding cities and counties.

The media will be your best avenue for communicating information about any potential problems. There is an AM radio station which the DOT has access to. You will be able to alert the public to tune-in to this station for periodic traffic reports. News media can also assist in letting the public know about changes in traffic patterns or parking lot availability. Television networks are another great source for the distribution of information.

This map is indicative of a signage plan that communicates which parking lots are designated for which type of parking pass.

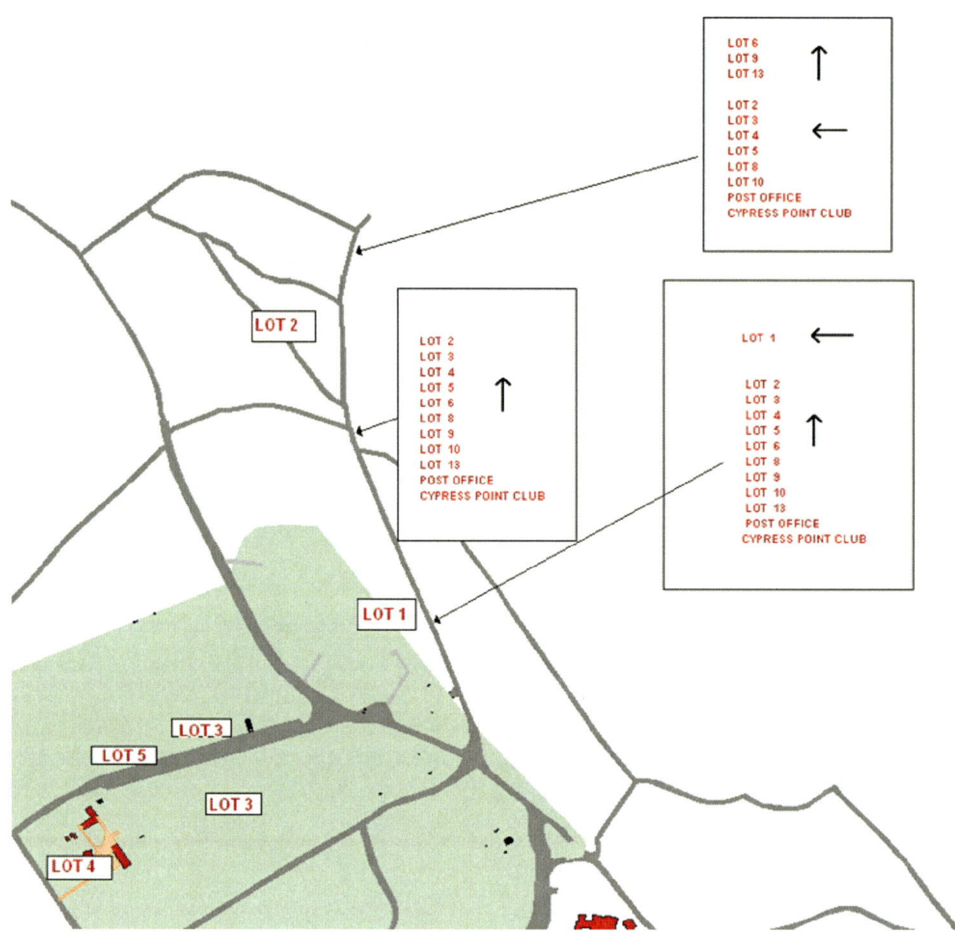

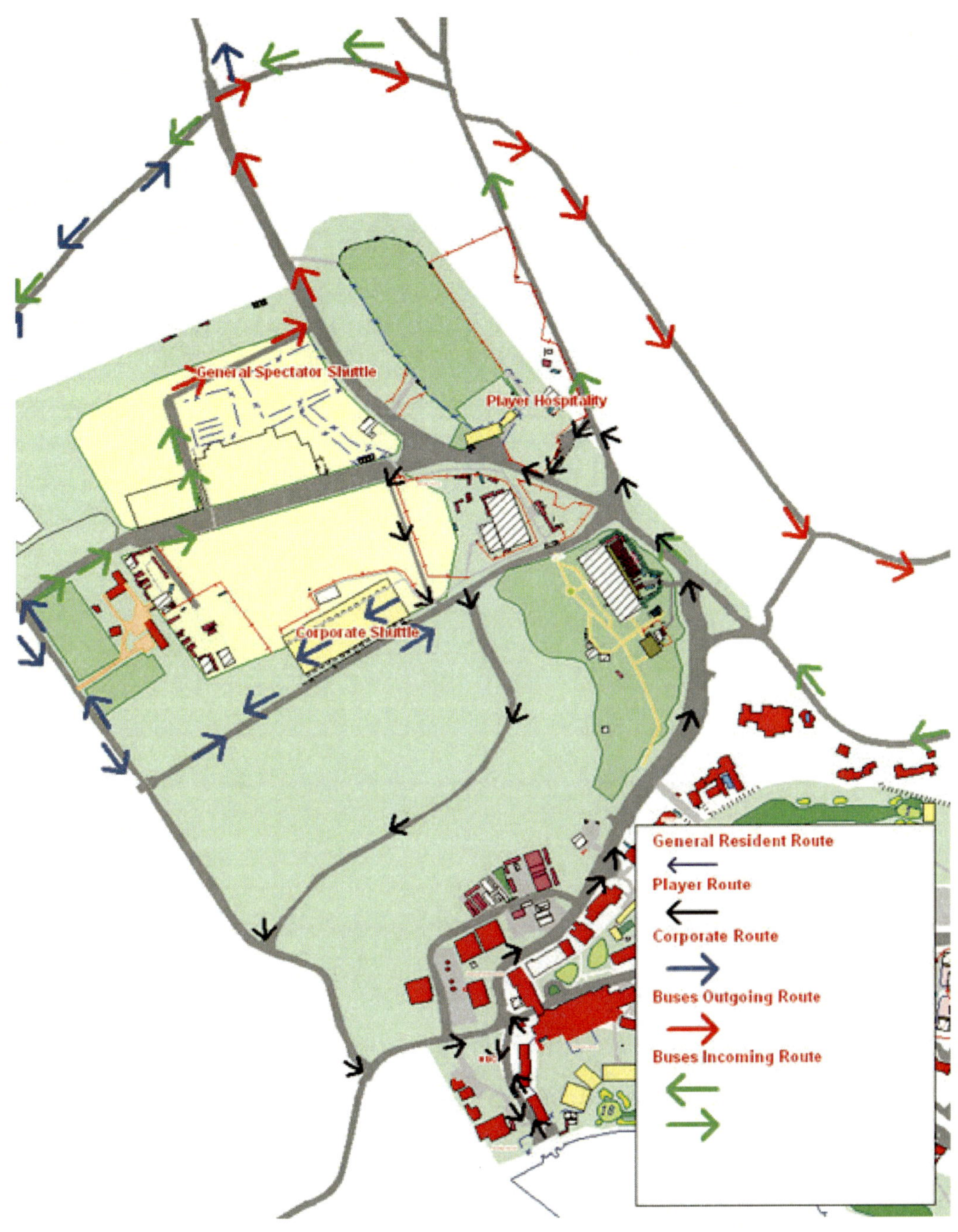

The legend of this map says it all. It illustrates the various routes each group takes. Try to keep the groups on separate routes to minimize traffic delays.

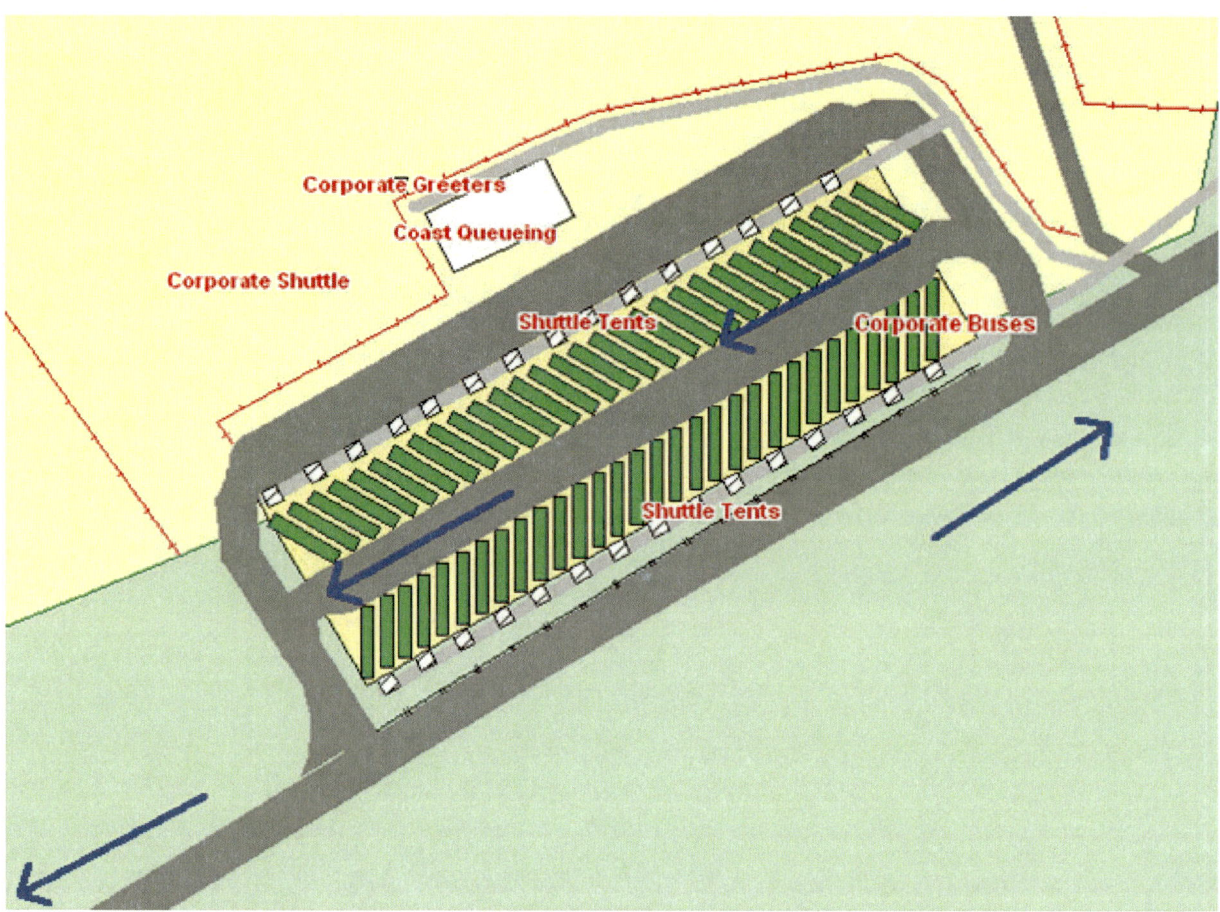

This is an example of a corporate bus depot. Corporations contract two or three buses to bring clients to and from the event. Bus staging areas are shown where the bus parks diagonally, in front of the area where the clients wait in queue to depart. Tents or awnings are provided, under which spectators may stand.

It is important not to allow too many buses to access the area at the same time. It may be necessary to create intervals between buses to allow more buses to drop and pick up at the same location.

This diagram designates the parking lots and the routes into the lots. It also illustrates the various shuttles and their pick up and drop off locations. This map was invaluable to the traffic department in determining their coverage points on the roads.

Drawings are always helpful when trying to make a point. People seem to understand concepts better when visually depicted.

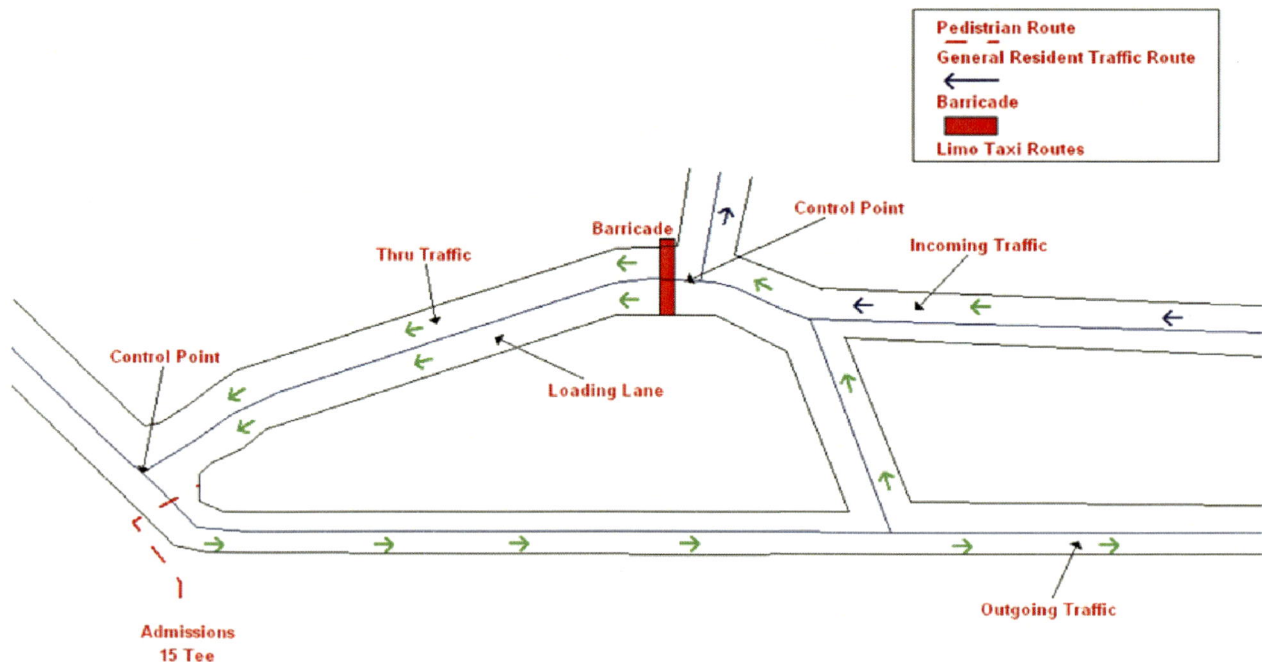

This diagram illustrates a taxi/limo drop-off route. It was drawn freehand withhin the mapping program.

It is necessary to provide the local taxi companies and limousine drivers directions to the drop-off area. This diagram illustrates where to stage to pick up passengers. A drop-off/pick up area needs to be provided for any event.

Chapter Sixteen

CORPORATE

Potential locations for various corporate venues have been discussed. At any event the best possible locations are selected for the corporate hospitality villages, as the revenue generated by corporate tents are often based upon location. Prime locations would be around the clubhouse, active fairways, around the driving range or putting green. That is not to say villages cannot be in other areas, but the same amount of revenue won't be generated in non-prime areas.

Depending upon the event the amount of corporate packages available and what they entail can be staggering. Each is designed to attract the most clients at the most return on the money spent. It may include pages in the program, banners, name on a sponsor board, signs throughout the event and the list goes on. The more items available in the package the higher the cost to be charged.

The size of the tent will also be an indicator of what the tent is worth. Size determines the number amount of people which can access the tent. In other words a 40'x40' tent may no matter how prime the location. If the venue is located in a depressed economic zone, the size of the tent will need to be cut down to be affordable. In other words a 40'x40' tent may accommodate over one hundred people, but if it is priced too high, it won't be sold, no matter how prime the location.

Tents need to have level flooring unless the ground is so even that contour flooring may be used. If there are any doubts, go with level flooring as clients are paying a great deal of money for the tents, you don't want the drinks sliding off the tables!

In all probability there will be a patio deck in front of each tent and perhaps a wood walkway in front of the patio to accommodate rainy conditions.

This is an example of flooring which is used for the corporate tent patios as well as the walkway between the tents.

The location and size of the tents has been established. Now make sure the ancillary items that need to go within each village can fit. Restroom trailers, generators, storage areas and dumpsters all need to be accommodated. There needs to be a road or cart access behind the tent in order to reach the facilities. As discussed in other chapters, if an area can't be serviced, you're in big trouble.

This is an example of the back of a corporate village.

Notice the four-ton air conditioners tucked between the tents. The smaller tents behind the main tents are for food preparation. There is a generator off to the left and storage boxes for the corporate clients to store miscellaneous material. The rock road is shown between facilities for access.

The interior of each tent needs to have a standard package, something included in the basic price. This could be air conditioning and heat, ceiling liner, lighting, tables and chairs, table cloths, restricted phone service, televisions and a sign identifying the user. Other standard amenities will include a determined number of tickets or passes, and parking privileges.

There might be other options offered to corporate client such as additional tickets, an upgraded tent interior; perhaps even a golf outing for their clients. Naturally, some of these options are at an additional cost. There are often events where some of the corporate hospitality is in the clubhouse.

Due to the desirable location, you may be able to charge a premium.

Generally speaking, there are not a lot of clubhouses large enough to handle the membership in conjunction with other hospitality. That being said, another reason to provide the membership with another space outside the clubhouse, any space within the clubhouse can be sold at premium price.

At some point the corporate clients want to know the locations and numbers of parking passes. In addition, if the parking areas cannot accommodate all of their parking needs they will want to know the location where they can shuttle the remainder of their clients.

These questions and more are normally covered in corporate update sessions held throughout the year prior to the event. Over the years, corporations who attend events have become quite savvy with their questions and requests. It is best to be prepared. Corporate Hospitality Services will be discussed in a later chapter.

There are other corporate revenue opportunities. A tent containing numerous tables designated by corporation is the most economical way for corporate clients to entertain. The food and beverage is included in the price so there are no surprises about cost. Generally, this is a lower much lower priced alternative to an individual tent. Drawbacks include fewer numbers of tickets per day and no choice in the menu provided.

If one table isn't enough, the client could always purchase more than one table. As with the corporate tents, a limited number of parking passes to a preferred location is included in this package.

Providing power for the standard tent packages is very easy as you know what you are providing in the package. The corporate client may have special power needs which you will need to address in advance.

Providing additional power is generally not a problem as long as these needs are articulated and planned for far enough in advance. The same holds true for additional phone service.

Additional phone capability in each village has been planned, but the client can't wait until the last minute to decide about special phone service; you may not be able to accommodate their request.

Servicing the corporate clients would require a chapter by itself as the intricacies of client management are very detailed and require professional staffing. This is not an area you want to have inexperience people involved in.

Landscaping for the villages and as other areas will be discussed in a subsequent chapter.

Chapter Seventeen

THE AMERICANS WITH DISABILITIES ACT (ADA)

It became a new world on the golf course when the Americans with Disabilities Act (ADA) was signed into law on July 26, 1990. It is a civil rights law – first and foremost. Although many look at it as a building code, this act is designed to ensure that individuals with disabilities (people with mobility, vision, hearing and other disabilities) have equal access to places, goods, services and events just like everyone else.

Visiting a different golf club each year presents its own set of challenges. Having to build a city for 50,000 people a day is the first challenge. Building structures (tents for corporate, merchandise, concessions) on a variety of elevations and terrain brings out the creativity, as does adding accessible port-a-johns, accessible entrances, mapping out routes for scooters, wheelchairs and multi-passenger golf carts. Then the final (and often most difficult) piece is finding grandstands where you can create ADA wheelchair seat locations.

When you have all of that figured out – you've just begun the process. It is imperative to construct your facilities to comply with the ADA Standards. The ADA Standards (these are Federal Regulations) are minimum standards.

That being said there are ways to mitigate situations with what would be reasonable accommodation. For example, not all concessions need to be ADA compliant due to existing surrounding elevation. You are not required to bulldoze land to accommodate ADA requirements.

Often times, you will be working under the oversight of a local, municipal or state code official. They want to know what your accessibility plans are. Most code officials review under the International Building Code (IBC) and the American National Standards Institute (ANSI A.117).

These are not the same as the ADA, and a code official cannot review and sign off on plans or provide an occupancy permit under the ADA. There are differences between building codes and ADA. Do your homework or engage a knowledgeable consultant who can help you navigate the differences.

Once you've created your plans, make sure that you can build what you've designed on at the locations identified. For example, a concession stand needs to have a level platform in front of the concession with a ramp leading onto the platform.

The ramp needs to have no greater fall or rise than 1:12, so if your platform is four inches off the ground, you must have a ramp that is four feet long.

Again, the requirement is one foot of ramp run for every one inch of ramp rise (1:12). It will be important to select locations where barriers are as minimal as possible. Making it safe and usable for someone in a wheelchair will benefit individuals who use walkers, canes, parents pushing baby strollers and can often prevent trip and fall accidents.

It will save you headaches in the long run.

Inside your facilities (corporate tents, merchandise pavilions, concessions) you need to make sure people can reach service tables, counters, bars, displays of goods, fitting rooms and other publicly accessible features. Once constructed at the correct levels you need to make sure these areas don't become another area

to store things, preventing it from being used by someone who cannot reach the higher bar.

Handrails on stairs and ramps are very important. They provide stability for individuals who walk, as well guidance for individuals with visual disabilities. Periodically check the condition of the ramps and handrails to keep them safe and functional.

ADA compliant temporary rest rooms present a unique challenge. Most, if not all, of the manufactured trailer rest rooms all have steps which can't be used by someone with a disability, so they are not ADA compliant. The alternative is an ADA compliant portopot, which provides a wider door, a larger area and grab bars around the toilet. What they don't typically provide is any way to wash your hands. The best addition you can request of the vendor is to install hand sanitizers in the ADA portopots.

Lastly, grandstand viewing areas for the event should be considered the critical component of ADA wheelchair seating. These areas need to be located in front of the grandstand where no one can stand in front of the spectator in a wheelchair. The wheelchair user must have an "unobstructed view" of what on the golf action.

Selecting grandstand locations where there is sufficient space to build an ADA compliant ramp up to the grandstand are the first challenge. Golf courses are not known for being flat. Place viewing areas where it is will be easy for people with disabilities to access. Sections across the front of the grandstand (separate and in front of where the other spectators are walking to their seats) is the next piece of the compliance equation. You need to have at least one companion seat/chair next to each ADA seat.

Although there is no set formula for the number and location of wheelchair and companion seats in grandstands, it will be important to have as many as you can. For a golf tournament, ADA grandstands at holes # 1, # 9 and # 18 are always the most popular. However due to uneven terrain it may not be feasible to provide access to these locations, so have alternative options available.

To support the needs of spectators with disabilities there should be a Disabled Services Committee comprised of volunteers. For a large event it could take more than 100 volunteers to monitor and transport people with disabilities. Golf courses are large, long and a challenge to traverse for virtually anyone.

Providing on-course transportation becomes a vital component of the Operations Department, working closely with the Disabled Services Volunteers.

That being said, there will be events that will limit the access due to the terrain and lack of accessible routes.

Many tournaments and events provide motorized scooters for use by spectators to travel around the course. There is usually no charge for the use of scooters and they are provided on a first-come, first-serve basis. The scooter vendor takes responsibility for getting spectators to sign release forms, provides instructions on the use of the scooter as well as what the driver should not try to do with the scooter (not that they always listen, of course), and typically requires photo identification to ensure the return of the scooter at the end of the visit.

For the past several years, the availability of longer multi-passenger golf carts with a flat area and a ramp in the middle has enabled a wheelchair user to come directly onto the cart in their wheelchair and be transported around the course. These are a welcomed addition for people trying to carry a wheelchair on the back of a golf

cart (not a good idea).

Here are some important points to remember in your attempts to provide an enjoyable experience for spectators with disabilities:•Remember that the ADA is about equal treatment, not special treatment. People with disabilities come in all shapes, sizes, colors and attitudes, just like everyone else. Don't be surprised or offended if someone with a disability demands that you do something (like carry their wheelchair, provide assistance in the rest room, etc.) because the "ADA says so."

An individual's demand doesn't mean it's true.

Sometimes, the best response starts with "I'm sorry", and continues with "we're not trained to (lift you onto the toilet, carry your wheelchair, etc.) and if we try to do that, you and I will both be injured. (President,Joan Stein Consulting LLC, 2011)"

If it doesn't sound right, trust your instincts. But best practice is to make sure that someone on the team (staff, consultant, etc.) is knowledgeable about the ADA and its requirements and can help to diffuse the situation before it gets out of control.

•If someone has a request, such as bringing a bag larger than allowed which contains needed medical equipment, etc., listen to the request. Use good judgment in treating these on a case-by-case basis.

•If someone with a disability is violating a clearly stated rule (such as no cell phones, no fighting, etc.) don't allow yourself to be bullied into allowing the rules to be ignored simply because of their disability – remember it's about equal treatment.

On July 26, 2010, the US Department of Justice adopted the first revised Rules and Regulations in 20 years. Some of the new rules focus on golf courses, which were never addressed in the original regulations. Many of the new requirements relate specifically to providing access to players with disabilities, not spectators.

We have come a long way and we should continue to evolve in this area, but there will
always be things you can and can't do. I keep coming back to reasonable accommodation, meaning that it is not always possible to follow the ADA standards explicitly due to the temporary environment you are creating.

A good consultant can help you steer clear of many problems in this area.

Chapter Eighteen

Other Hospitality Venues

Depending on the arrangements made with major vendors for high cost items, separate hospitality may be provided to these vendors to help defray costs. These hospitality tents may need to be larger than the norm and located in more elite areas depending upon the extent of the deal. Make sure there is enough space carved out on site to accommodate the needs. In some cases, tent space in one of your existing villages may be used if there is not another area available.

At some events, if located at a club, a member tent may be required to accommodate the members who have been displaced from the clubhouse. This tent is normally in close proximity to the clubhouse to give the members the feeling that they are not being displaced too far. Give thought to the location as air conditioning or heat and well as a power source need to be provided. Normally a food prep area behind the tent and a bar inside the tent are needed. Access to the tent should not interfere with the other activities which surround the clubhouse. Hospitality for the event organizers should also be provided. If the clubhouse, due to lack of space, can't accommodate the number of clients to be entertained, a large tent will be needed. The same space requirements as the member tent are required. As part of this package you may offer other amenities such as day trips or golf privileges at other courses close by.

Décor options will be discussed later.

Player hospitality is usually located inside the clubhouse, if at all possible, close to the locker room to enhance security. Depending upon the size of the event, it might be possible to have player hospitality, player family hospitality, players' lounge and locker room all in the clubhouse.

This is generally the best situation; however, there are times that the clubhouse is too small to accommodate these needs and a player compound must be created. The compound would include a player hospitality tent, player parking area and possibly, locker room facilities. It doesn't really matter whether the facilities are in a clubhouse or in a player compound as long as it is convenient and the players are safe.

You need to be able to provide safe passage for the players when they interact or cone in contact with the spectators. This interaction would occur as the players leave their compound to go the range, putting green, media tent, scoring areas, tees and leaving greens.

Parking will be a major concern for all the groups mentioned. Player parking is usually somewhere on site where players are protected from the public. Some VIP parking also is traditionally on site or at the very least, close to the site in a preferred location. It is impossible to accommodate all of the VIP parking requests for on- site parking due to space restraints, but a dedicated shuttle is often provided for these people.

These areas should have been discussed during facility placement in the initial planning phase.

Chapter Nineteen

DÉCOR

This area can become quite extensive as well as expensive. The size of the event will generally dictate the level and intricacy of interior design. Décor may include a general theme for the event incorporating flags, banners, tent treatments, facades, and color schemes.

We have already discussed the standard décor package for corporate tents, but upgraded décor packages can be as lavish as the budget affords. The client can start with a colored ceiling liner; add draperies or hard walls for a simple effect. There is a wide assortment of seating plans, bars, lighting packages; the imagination is the only limit: besides the cost. A theme may be chosen and everything constructed in the tent will mirror the rendering provided. The choice of carpet or hard wood floors can continue the theme. There will be other areas which will need dressing up.

In this particular corporate tent, the upgrades include television cubes, hard columns, chair covers, glass tables and wall draperies.

These photos illustrate examples of more elaborate décor upgrades.

Your décor vendor will also be responsible for the large tents. The corporate table tent can hold as many as 200 tables, but you don't want it to look like an aircraft hangar. The same is true for the upgraded ticket tent. Both of these tents can be as large as 30,000 square feet, which is huge by anyone's terms.

The décor vendor has used color and columns to break up the large space so it is not so cavernous. The event needs to have a feeling of continuity and the décor package should include the color theme throughout.

The color theme may be incorporated into the event logo and complimented by the placement of flags and banners in appropriate areas of the site.

The color theme will also be used inside the tents with accents that complement the presentation. In some locations facades may be added to unify a group of tents or to set off a location as a point of importance such as the main admissions gate. Make sure they are installed at a height which cannot be reached. If banners are hung too low, most of them will be missing overnight, as they make great souvenirs.

Take care in the placement of the flags and banners. If they are placed in remote locations you may find them missing in the morning. The number of flags and banners is really a personal choice only limited by budget. You can blanket the property or only highlight specific areas.

Work with the décor provider to decide what you want in the other hospitality venues. Give the vendor a budget to work with. Otherwise his first presentations will waste time, because the cost will be excessive.

The general rule would be to maximize space for seating and service, paying attention to the amount of exits required the fire marshal, but giving the effect and ambiance desired.

The décor company usually needs an abundance of time to prepare the tent interiors, based upon the number of upgrades the clients have chosen. This will impact the set-up timeline so stay on top of it. Remember, if the décor company isn't on time, no one will be. What they are doing impacts other vendors.

Other considerations would be compound space as discussed during facility placement and the interaction with the fire marshal. If your vendor plans to provide dining tents using propane you will need the fire marshal's approval.

If the décor vendor plans to use combustible materials in the compound during the construction of the décor items, the fire marshal will insist these materials meet flame retardant codes. These specifications should be readily available.

It is easy to get out of hand and over budget when dealing with décor. While you want the site to look the best it can, never lose sight of the fact that the spectators are going to the event to see the event.

After the last ball has been struck, the décor vendor will begin tearing down immediately, so it is best to be prepared by having vendor meetings prior to the event to decide on the tear-out schedule.

Chapter Twenty

Landscaping

Similar to décor, a great deal of money can be spent on landscaping. Set a budget for each area to be landscaped.

Unfortunately, sometimes it takes a great deal of landscaping to make an area look presentable. Concentrate on defined areas such as corporate villages, admission gates, media facilities, and player facilities, other hospitality areas, concessions on course, portable restroom enclosures and any other areas which the spectators might frequent.

Having established a budget, it needs to be incorporated into a written scope of work.

The scope of work is integrated into a bid package and sent to prospective landscapers.
Obviously, you have done your homework as far as researching the local or national landscapers who have the ability to do the job on a timely and cost efficient basis.

Included in the bid package is a request for a timeline to accomplish their proposed landscape, a breakdown of the plant material, the number of people required to get the job done on time, equipment requirements, and watering requirements.

Once all the bid prices have been received, a meeting is scheduled to review the scope with each vendor. Examine what each landscaper is providing for the money. You want assurances that they can get the job done; knowing that landscaping will be one of the last things to be completed prior to the start of the event. The vendor will need to know that long work days and weekends if necessary are the norm. Whatever it takes to finish the job on time is paramount to the success of the event. In turn, the vendor should articulate his needs and expectations, whether it is location of water for the plants to golf carts for access.

Sometimes, the amount of landscape for the money is pitiful; other times it is substantial. If you are finding that the available money to spend on landscaping isn't going very far, then you may need to concentrate your efforts on fewer areas and do a bigger splash where you can.

This picture shows the beginning of a landscaped area. Notice how the ground is protected with filter cloth. This will make it easier to pick up the plants and mulch after the event.

These are examples of landscaping in front of corporate tents and along the walkway.

Everything is in containers, but hidden nicely.

Landscape companies take their work very seriously and do not want their name on something that won't look good. After everything is installed, it is not uncommon for the landscaper to come back and add material to fill out an area.

Pride can work in your favor here. Once the landscaper has an idea of the site, they are normally very self-sufficient and will only contact you if there are questions or problems to solve.

The landscaper's compound can fit along fence lines off one of the roads you have constructed. Access to the compound comes from the road and the fence can be used to hang baskets, as long as there is a nearby water supply. Incorporate landscaping into the timeline knowing that they will be one of the last vendors to start on the property. If allowed to start too early, then the plant material will likely be crushed by other vendors trying to finish. If you start too late, they won't finish. It's a fine line to walk.

Watering the plant material is paramount. You will need to get with the superintendent early to establish where you can tap into a water source in all landscape locations. If it is not readily available, you may need to bring it in from another location. This can get expensive so plan on it early.

The plant beds will probably be mulched to hide the plant containers which create a clean look. Make sure there is a plan for removal of the mulch after the event. There needs to be an understanding of whether it will be stockpiled on site or needs to be hauled off. Sometimes the superintendent wants it, sometimes he doesn't.

At some events, the landscaper might ask to allow the general public to come into the site a few days following the end of the event to take whatever flowers they might want as they are going to die without water.

This can create other problems as the public tends to take everything not tied down. It also can create a liability issue with cars and pedestrians mixing with vendors who are trying to tear down the site.

A more acceptable practice would be to donate the plant material to charitable groups which would greatly minimize the traffic picking up the plants.

If you are going to allow this to happen, you need to establish a specific procedure. Things are somewhat chaotic after the event ends and you may not want to contribute to the confusion by allowing the general public back on the property.

Chapter Twenty One

MERCHANDISE

This area has huge potential as a revenue source if managed by an experienced professional. This book will not address buying plans, garment selection, or fixture requirements.

We will discuss the operational areas pertinent to the merchandise.

The size of the tent is the first and foremost thing to consider. It would naturally be sized proportionately to the number of spectators expected for the event and the popularity of the venue. The marketing team will be able to assist by providing this information. Also, talk to people who have run similar events held in the area in order to get a feel for volume, flow, and spending habits.

The tent requires a level floor and the number of exits required by the fire marshal based upon the occupancy loads. It needs to be ADA compliant with ramps for ingress and egress. There should be a large enough area around the back of the tent to have a loading dock and storage trailers to hold the merchandise to be sold.

The tent should have good lighting and be fitted with air conditioning and heat. The layout should have enough room for an abundance of check-out stations and cash registers to move the spectators through the lines quickly and efficiently.

There will be a spider web of Cat 5 wires connecting the cash registers back to the transaction trailer allowing for high speed credit card transactions. There is a need for other phone installations to accommodate customer service and administration.

There will be a finance trailer to provide for the day's accounting and bank deposits, as well a restroom trailer for the volunteers and staff. A volunteer break tent and a volunteer check in trailer should also be provided.

A standard 30-yard dumpster and cardboard compactor will be necessary to keep this area operating efficiently and cleanly.

Generally, there will ATMs located close to the merchandise entrance as well a package check tent and shipping tent close by. A package check tent is for articles purchased at the merchandise tent that the spectator doesn't want to carry around all day while watching the event. The items can be picked up at the end of the day. The shipping tent is for articles purchased that may be too large or delicate to pack in a suitcase and need to be shipped home.

More specifically, the loading dock area behind the merchandise tent should accommodate at least twenty two tractor trailers full of merchandise or as many as you can fit behind the tent to support the operation through the event. The merchandise director will let you know how many trailers are needed.

This can be a challenge if you are dealing with uneven terrain. A normal tractor trailer has a floor height four feet above level ground. If the terrain is uneven, some trailers floors will be below a level loading dock as others will be above the dock.

Under adverse conditions, such as these, you may find yourself building a series of loading docks of different configurations to accommodate the four-foot height of the trailers. There will need to be ramps to allow push carts to access the main tent once the merchandise is off-loaded from the trailers. In order to place all the storage trailers you may need to construct some temporary access roads if the storage area is located on grass. This is necessary as the tractor cabs used to set the tractors are mainly used for highway driving and do not have much power off road, especially if the ground is damp. These tractor cabs only have two axles as opposed to bigger tractor cabs which have four axles. It all comes down to enough power to pull the trailers in less than perfect conditions.

The merchandise tent may be highly elevated off the ground, in some locations possibly eight feet or more due to the unevenness of the ground. Entrance and exit ramps must comply with ADA specifications. Depending upon the space available you might be able to build such ramps or not. If not, it will be necessary to rent a portable elevator suitable for the job.

The only positive thing about tents high off the ground is the installation of the wiring. Installers can walk under the tent to do their jobs. However the cost of a tent rose to this height is very expensive. I would suggest trying to do some grading of the ground, if possible, to reduce the height.

This is an example of the merchandise tent construction. Due to the extreme size once the floor is constructed, the center section of the floor must be removed to allow the boom lift access to raise the heavy tent frame. The weight of the boom lift will cause ruts on the grass, so you should place thick plywood down to minimize the damage. Notice this was not done in this example and paid the price for the oversight. Once the tent frame has been raised the center section of floor will be re-installed.

The merchandise tent construction timeline is normally tight since the facility opens prior to the main event.

The merchandise area will need to be restricted so the public only has access to the tent and back out to the parking or shuttle pick up locations. This can be accomplished with bike rack fencing as it is easy, albeit time consuming, to install.

There should be portable toilets available and the ATM should be stocked and ready to go. The parking lot for the sale should have already been established, staffed with attendants to direct the patrons to the correct areas for parking as well as the access to the merchandise tent. There may also be some traffic cops on the road if the sale is expected to impact traffic.

In addition, there will be contract security to make sure no one wanders away from the merchandise area. The sale is a great source of revenue, but it is also disruptive to your vendors who may have to find other routes around the site due to the congestion in the area.

When the event is over, if all goes well, all of the merchandise is sold out. If there are some items left, then there may be another sale, which causes the same amount of heartache, sometimes more. At this point all of the vendors are rushing to get off the site and it is hard to distinguish the patron from the vendor if they are wandering around the site.

This is truly a dangerous situation. There will be a large number of forklifts running around the site picking up heavy material as well as large trucks vying for different areas of the site to pick up their wares.

With the amount of heavy equipment on site and the public who are not always paying attention to what is going on around them, you will want to segregate the two as much as possible. Give a great deal of thought to pre and post-sale logistics and be sure to keep the patrons separated from the vendors at all costs Additional security will be helpful during this time.

Chapter Twenty Two

MEDIA

We have discussed the size of the media compound in a previous chapter but the space may be greatly reduced depending upon the size of the venue. It some cases there is a large working media tent holding up to 350 working press(possibly more), outfitted with telephones, televisions, scoreboards, work tables, faxes and copiers and a large registration area. Combined with this tent would be additional tents for the interview area and dining area. A food prep tent would be attached to the dining tent.

In some instances the working media tent and interview tent may be combined into one tent provided the noise levels aren't too high. The dining tent is normally a separate space but can be combined with the others depending upon the space needed.

During the planning phase the number of telephones necessary for this area is determined. Cable is normally brought to a back board located behind the scoreboard and the phone cable is run to each work space. During this time any special phone and video needs are explored to make sure accommodations have been allowed. The communications company will normally add 50 or 60 lines, in addition to what has been ordered, to be safe. Media people inherently do not order phone lines in advance, but still expect them to be available. Be proactive and plan ahead.

Plan to have 25 lines active over the amount actually ordered and ready to go for these last minute stragglers. These requirements have been revised and reduced in most cases due to technological advances over the years.

Air conditioning and heat are provided necessitating additional space outside the tent for air handlers and generators.

In addition, there are a number of office trailers present, all of which lend support to the media operation.

Restroom facilities need to be located in a convenient location to the main working media tent. A photographer's lounge, where the photographers can house their equipment, should be provided and include lockable lockers. Don't forget about the water needed for the restroom trailers. This should have been included in the construction as part of the plumbing requirements.

Attention needs to be given to landscape needs and any banners or flags to dress out the tent.

Parking areas and shuttle systems need to be thought out to give the media convenient access to the venue. Media often spend long hours in the media tent writing their stories, so any so any convenience is usually appreciated. The shuttle schedule to the event will normally be two or three coach buses running from their parking lot first thing in the morning until around 11:30 am. By this time most of the media will be on site and you can switch to van shuttles until around 4:30 pm or 5:00 pm when coach buses will be utilized again until around 10:00 pm.

After 10:00 pm one bus should be able to handle the load easily. Depending upon the size of the event and the location of the media lot, the whole shuttle process should be handled with vans, but do the homework to make sure. Upon occasion there may be enough room on-site to accommodate media parking.

During the weeks prior to the event, media will be seeking information for stories about a multitude of things: course set-up, corporate clients and the like. It is best to forward all requests to the media director to let him handle or facilitate response. This is crunch tine and you have enough to do without the distractions.

Most media directors are very happy to help you get the word out concerning the many facets of the event which are necessary for the spectators' well-being, ranging from parking and traffic to weather issues.

Over the years the media has become very picky about the food offered in the dining area, whether they pay for it or it is provided complimentary.

The Media Director will provide the access passes required to select media to attend the event. It is possible for cell phone Video walls at the front of the media center require projectors to be installed closer to the entrance and it is a fine line trying to place the truss work between tables and entry points without causing a disruption of traffic flow. You still need to maintain room for height of the truss work and stability to hold the projectors. It all cases the truss work penetrates through the floor to the ground below at least three feel to hinder the trusses from tipping over. Anything less and you are inviting trouble and may require guide wires to hold the trusses upright.

There will most certainly be a need for a vehicle to take the players from the 18th green to the media tent for interviews unless it is located in close proximity and the players can walk without being disturbed by spectators.

Cell phones and radios need to be included for the tournament media staff.

Meet with the media director to insure you have met all of his requirements for the on-site setup. Make sure there are enough power outlets at each work station. There should be an abundance of trash receptacles in the tent and assigned personnel to maintain a clean working environment throughout the event. High speed internet access or wireless routers should be provided for media use. High speed is mandatory these days.

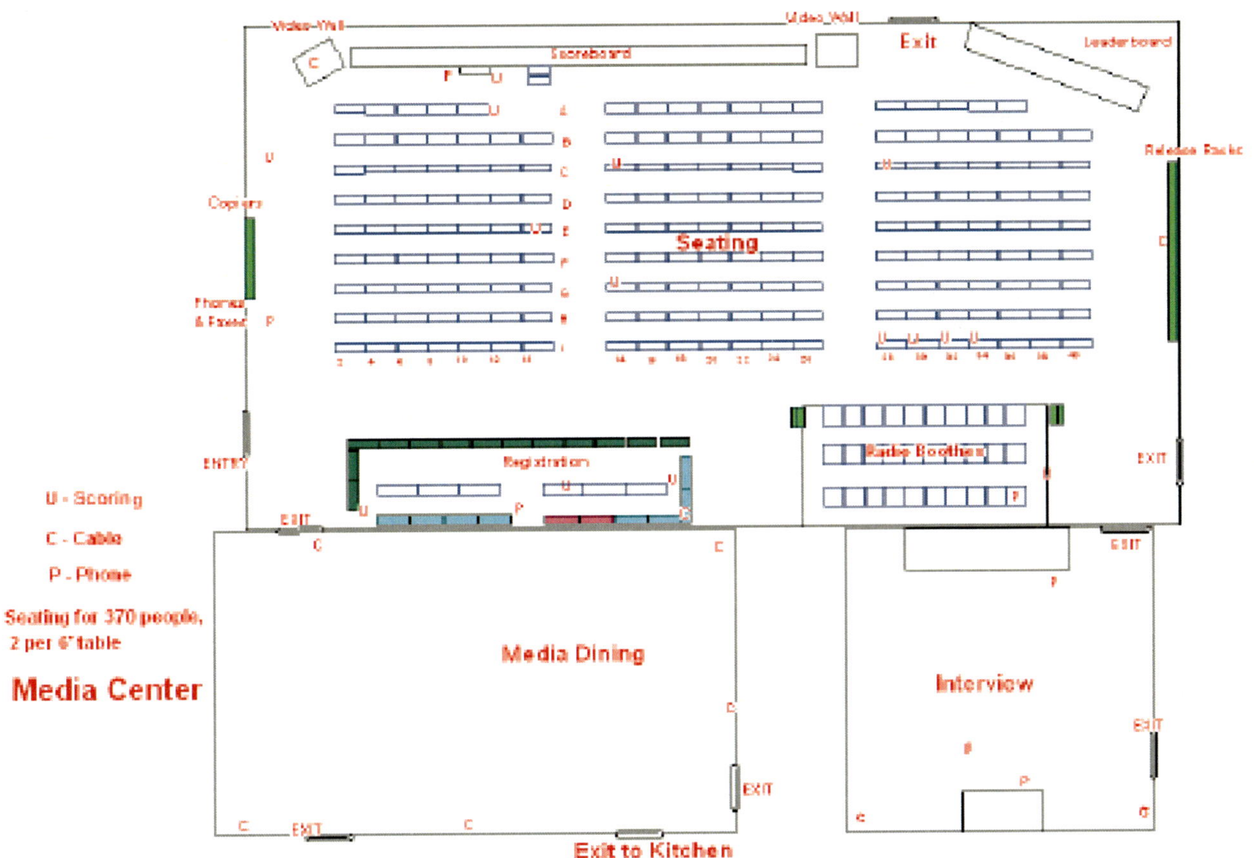

This is an example of a typical media center layout. It shows three separate areas. The main tent is where the working media write and file their stories during the event. Media dining is where the media eat during the day and evening. The interview tent is where the players are interviewed following their round.

The size of these facilities depends upon the size of your event and the number of media covering it.

Chapter Twenty Three

CONCESSIONS

Since food and beverage have the potential of being a good revenue source particular attention should be given to this operation.

Pick the best vendor from those who have had experience working in this environment and have demonstrated that they serve a quality product. Based upon these requirements you can negotiate commission percentages, menus and prices.

Walk the site with the concessionaire to pick the best available locations for the spectators to access tents. This may not be as easy as you might think; you have to consider whether the locations will be seen on camera while the venue is in operation. There needs to be enough room not only for the size tent you want, but the support facilities that go with each tent, such as waste water holding tanks, hand wash stations, propane and dumpsters for the garbage. It will need to be determined whether potable water is an issue at each location if required.

Concessions require a great deal of staffing and for food service to work there needs to be a seamless method for employees to access the site to get to work. Concession staffing may consist of local civic groups, church groups, school teachers or any other volunteer organization. The groups are paid a commission based upon the sales they generate in exchange for the labor to run the concessions.

The number of people needed to run the concession stands can range up to 800 or 1000 depending on the number of concessions and the expected attendance. The credentialing process for the concession staff is normally a daily ticket distributed outside the admission gates at a tent. This alleviates the problem and expense of trying to track down a worker if they have decided to go wandering. If food service workers are to use the general spectator shuttle they need to be assured that the buses will run on time otherwise there will be no one to serve the food.

If you are serving alcoholic beverages, a time needs to be established as to when such service will be cut off every day.

Training of staff in this area is extremely important. All health department guidelines must be met and the serving staff adequately trained in the proper procedure of handling food as well as interaction with the spectators.

Make sure the concessionaire and the health department connect with each other early in the planning process. They will need to discuss health code issues well in advance. This will hold true for the fire marshal who will definitely enforce stringent guidelines for the storage of propane. Training classes should be conducted by the concessionaire for the food and beverage staff.

Weather will play a big part in the success of a concession operation. If the weather is cold then sales will suffer; if the weather is hot then you will see an increase in sales of cold liquid beverages. Unfortunately, the weather is one thing out of our control.

Access roads or paths need to be available for the restocking of the tents as well as for the removal of garbage and waste water. The tents used for the concessions must match the other tents on site to maintain the theme and continuity of the site.

They should be inviting to the public and the menu boards should be large enough to be read easily. The sign boards should have a professional look and clip on letters should never be used. The concessions should be designed for speed of service and efficiency to capture maximum sales. Counter height should be constructed to accommodate ADA requirements. There should be a stabilized surface in front of the concession tents extending 20 feet out to avoid a muddy mess when it rains.

Landscape and banners will add another nice touch.

Generally speaking, the more concessions available for the general spectator to frequent, the better the potential revenue.

Whether the concession compound is located on-site or off, there will be some things on-site the concessionaire will need access to throughout the day. A 53 foot ice truck and a few 30 foot beer trucks will need to be located somewhere on site where they can be accessed as necessary.

The water distribution committee will need to pick up ice from the ice truck to cool the water on the tees, so you will need to work out a procedure to keep track of the number of bags used. This will insure the concessionaire is paid for the ice taken.

Chapter Twenty Four

CATERING

Catering affords another potential high-end profit center as catering mainly involves corporate clients and tents.

Again, select this vendor the same way as the food concessionaire. You need to be assured that they can handle the volume as well as maintain the highest quality and service standards. Check references carefully to make sure they have experience with an event of this magnitude. It would be helpful to attend an event for which they are catering to get a feel for their operation. Some caterers are willing to pay more commission if the event picks up some of the hard costs such as tents, tables, chairs and linen rentals.

Once the corporate tent villages have been established, the caterer needs to sit with the clients to determine the scope of menus needed for the length of the event. The menus vary from the elaborate to basic depending upon the clients' needs. The caterer knows what their hard costs are and what it will cost for each menu item. Menu prices will rise and fall depending upon the amount of commission the event wants to make. An example might be a menu item costs the caterer ten dollars including markup. The event wants to receive a 20% to the client on that item. The item would sell for twelve dollars.

Remember that.

The caterer will normally request space in each village for a mini compound which would consist of refrigerated and dry storage trucks and food prep tents behind every corporate chalet.

The caterer will have a main compound at some location on the property which will house the production kitchen, a loading dock with assorted refrigeration and dry storage trucks. The main kitchen will need potable water as hand sinks utilized in food preparation. Hot water heaters will also be in use so there will probably be a need for propane tanks to be stored around the tent. They will have a fleet of trucks for delivery to each village as well as a number of golf carts to get around during the event.

A warehouse will be necessary for receiving shipments during the event and for maintaining the correct inventory before allocating supplies to various areas.

There will need a place for employees to dine as well as a location for the restroom trailer. Hopefully there will be enough space in the compound for the parking of a few staff cars. The majority of the staff will park at the general admission lot and take a shuttle to the site. They may also take a train if you are providing shuttles from the train station.

The caterer will provide food for the players and also the other hospitality venues discussed in previous chapters. Staffing the catering operation is larger than the

concession operation and the training needs to be geared towards high-end food service. Normally, the staff for the catering operation is paid by the hour and the amount of staff is too large to use volunteer organizations.

The main goal of any catering operation is to make the food look as full at the end of the service periods as it did at the beginning. This means that the buffets should look fresh and have a wide assortment of food until the end of the serving period.

Personnel are often recruited from culinary institutes across the nation. Staffing can reach 1200 or more accounting for chefs, cooks, prep personnel, dish washers, servers, carvers, tent managers and administrators. The number of areas they need to serve will dictate the amount of staff necessary. The credential process will mirror that of the concessionaire. Normally all of the staff other than the cook staff will have daily tickets to maximize control. The cook staff will have badges produced.

The credentials will be distributed outside the admission gates.

The health department will play a large role with the caterer as food temperatures at temporary events are critical and it is not uncommon to see the officials checking temperatures in the food prep areas before the food is served to the clients.

The caterer may require an additional dry storage trailer at each of the villages as well as refrigeration trucks. Each event is different, so two trucks per area or up to six depending upon the size of each village may be needed. Ease of access to the village during the day is another factor to consider.

Include the caterer in the planning phase of the area around the villages to make sure they get what they need to perform at top-level.

Chapter Twenty Five

GRANDSTANDS

There are only a few bleacher or grandstand companies I would trust to install a safe and quality product for an event of this magnitude. That being said, you need to do your research on all the companies in your area. If you don't need a lot of bleachers, then a local vendor may be the way to go, however, if you need a large number of bleacher seats, then one of the national companies is a better option.

I had a problem with a bleacher company a few years ago. They were trying a new system of tip up seating for the first time. They were so far behind in the construction schedule that they neglected to install the handrails required by code for the certificate of occupancy from the building department. I had to act fast otherwise the bleachers would have been unusable until the violation was fixed. I hired a team of carpenters work overnight to install wooden dowels, at the proper dimensions, to the stair rails. They worked from 6pm and finished as the first ball of the event was being hit the next morning. While this is uncommon, you have to be able to assess the situation and arrive at a solution. This particular situation added some tense moments and a few gray hairs.

Conduct a site survey with the bleacher company to determine the number of seats which will fit comfortably at each proposed location. At this time discuss any problem trees. You are looking for a ratio of 1:2 when it comes to bleacher seats; one seat for every two people. This will allow more attendance for your event, as half the people will be in seats watching the event.

If this is a golf event, the bleachers need to be far enough from the green as to not interfere with play and become a rules problem. The bleacher contractor should be able to help you with entry and exit locations into the stands. Normally, the bleachers will start at a height of at least four feet above the ground to accommodate the people standing in front of the bleachers.

You don't want people standing which may block the views of the spectators in the stands. This would hold true for other types of events as well.

Also look to your bleacher company to build any temporary bridges you might need. There have been occasions when a temporary bridge has been constructed overnight to free up a congested cart path. Companies have also been called on to construct towers used in hanging nets at the ends of driving ranges. You will probably be constructing viewing areas for wheelchairs at select holes around the course, requiring platforms to be built. This would either fall to the bleacher company or the flooring vendor.

The compound space needed for the bleacher company is initially large, but it is usually barren by the time the event happens as all the equipment has been moved out to the course. An office trailer, as well as some portable toilets for the workers, should be provided. There will be a lot of trucks arriving with steel and wood for the stands, depending upon the numbers ordered, and most of the trucks will be unloaded in the bleacher compound and materials transported to the appropriate locations by fork lifts and hay wagons.

If you are lucky enough to have some spare room in the locations where the bleachers are placed, you can save some time by allowing the trucks to unload in these areas.

Make sure you have the room to spare and this action doesn't impact another vendor. Also make sure the club knows what you are doing as they may have a social event planned in that area of which you are not aware. Better to be safe than sorry. Once the steel is up the seat boards are installed and painted. Logo windscreen is then nailed to the front of the bleachers creating a clean look.

If you want a different look you can use tilt up seats instead of the bench type. These seats have backs and add a dramatic look to any location; however if you need more seats than you have space, stick with bench seats as tilt up requires more room for fewer seats. If there are locations that do not have road or path access the superintendent might help out by providing a turf tire tractor for the bleacher vendor to pull the hay wagon around.

The bleacher company will, in most cases, be responsible for the construction of the camera and announce towers throughout the course.

The announce towers are raised platforms situated by designated greens with tents built on top of them. Hard walls are built inside the tents to provide sound proofing and the announcers sit inside each constructed booth which has a plexiglass window facing the green. It is from these announce booths that the television talent from the networks comment on play throughout the telecast. It will be prudent to do the television survey at the same time as the bleacher survey to eliminate any conflicts which may arise between the two areas.

The announce tower will require the most space depending on the number of broadcast networks the event, so the survey should be sooner rather than later to make sure there is enough space for the towers and all associated facilities, such as portable restrooms, generators, air conditioning and golf carts.

The bleacher construction timeline is one which is the most flexible. The club may prefer you to wait to build the bleachers around the clubhouse until the end so there is less impact on the membership. There will be times that the course is too wet for the bleacher company to build in areas of the course, since they would have to travel across grass with a heavy forklift. During this time they may be able to work on other bleachers which are close to or right off a paved path.

Once the event is over the bleacher company will begin to remove the towers and bleachers, which is most important to the club. It will generally take a long time to dismantle and ship all of the materials off site and will require a large quantity of tractor trailers. The hardest part for the bleacher company is the contracting of the trucks necessary to ship the materials.

This is an example of a temporary bridge. Your event may need to have temporary bridges around the site to allow spectator access which doesn't impact the players.

Photos provided by T & B Equipment

This is an example of tip-up bleacher seats. It creates a stunning look from the middle of the fairway as you approach the green. The seats are comfortable and provide a good view. However, it requires more space to build tip up seats and provides less seats than standard bleacher seats in the same footprint.

Notice the windscreen in front of the bleachers.

This is an example of standard bleacher seats. It provides maximum seating capacity in the available space.

Chapter Twenty Six

FENCING

We have come into the age of tightened security at events which has required the fencing of the total site. This can be a great deal of fence depending upon the venue. Unless the fence is going through trees and is hidden from view there should be windscreen attached to the fence to make it less noticeable.

Fencing is also used to enclose dumpsters, vendor compounds, generators, driving range, special parking areas, and the behind the scenes at concessions, corporate villages, merchandise back of the house, media compound and portable toilet locations.

Some of the fence will have windscreen on it either with logos or without. Some will need to be of varying heights, ranging from four foot to ten foot depending on the location and purpose. Most of the areas fenced are to protect the contents.

Vendor compounds need fencing to keep unauthorized personnel from entering and removing construction materials. Generators are fenced to keep people away from the high voltage being generated. Corporate villages are fenced to keep out the people who do not have the correct access. The merchandise back of the house area is fenced to keep people from stealing merchandise. The driving range is fenced to keep people from running onto the range and stealing practice balls. Dumpsters and portopots are fenced and sometimes covered with windscreen to hide the unsightliness of the contents. Special parking areas are fence to insure unauthorized cars can't sneak into the lot. The media compound is fenced to deter the public from trying to sneak in to catch a view of a player.

A general rule would be if it is back of the house, use a type of fence so the area can't be seen. Based on what you have just read you can imagine how long it will take to put up this much fence and the number of crews working. The unfortunate part is that not all the fence can go up at the same time.

Long runs can be installed, but gaps need to be maintained until the last minute to allow for ease of access by other vendors still setting up. If you are fencing the perimeter of the golf course, the up. If you are fencing the perimeter of the golf course, the process can occur early as it has a low impact on the club.

Another type of fence used is called bike rack. It looks like the bike racks you see in front of schools, but it is free standing and is about four feet in height. It makes a good barrier when you are making walk ways for players between crowds or queuing areas for large quantities of people. It is easy to set up and take down, but like anything, if there are long runs to install, it can become tiresome quickly.

You will also need a large storage area for the bike rack as it arrives disassembled in racks. Once the bike rack is assembled and distributed, you will need to store the shipping racks somewhere out of the way.

The fence compound is generally one of the smallest as the materials are rolls of fence and pipes. The material, depending upon your contractor, goes up fast. You

will find that your fence contractor will be one of the last vendors to finish, through no fault of their own, due to the amount of time they have to wait for other vendors to finish before they can seal up the area.

Make sure you call a utility locating company if you don't want fence pipe pounded through underground wires, conduit or pipe. This can be an expensive and dangerous lesson if it happens.

It is amazing to see how many places will require fencing after you thought you were finished. Just be aware, because it will happen. In choosing the vendor, make sure the company understands the changing nature and project scope. If they are too rigid about the installation schedule and unable to adapt to the changing nature of the event, they will never survive.

We have found it beneficial to use two fence vendors since our scope is so large. One is generally used for all the offsite installations at the parking lots inclusive of bike rack for spectator queuing at the bus staging areas and another vendor for everything on site.

The last minute additions would be too hard for one vendor to handle if they had to travel to all the parking lots in addition to the onsite changes. In some extreme situations we have had a third vendor responsible solely for the installation of all the bike rack. This frees up your operations crew to do other things.

This vendor, in particular, needs to understand that they just cannot come onto the site, put up all the fence and leave. It just doesn't happen that way. There will be times during the event, that additional fence may be added to improve the spectator traffic flow. Similarly, fence may be taken down during the event for the same reason.

If this is made clear during the bid review process, you can avert a lot of problems down the road.

Chapter Twenty Seven

SIGNS

There will be an abundance of signs of different types necessary in locations throughout the venue.

The signs on-site will need to direct the spectators to areas of interest such as the merchandise tent, concessions, restroom facilities, clubhouse, driving range, putting green, corporate villages, information kiosks, security headquarters and medical locations. These will be trail blaze signs and are normally located at the entrance gates, crosswalks, concessions and mainly anywhere else spectators are traveling.

An example of this type might be a painted four foot by four foot post driven into the ground with two inch by eight inch boards nailed to all four sides of the post with directions to various points of interest in two inch letters. The height of the last sign nailed to the post must be high enough that a person won't hit their head on it when walking under the signs. It's important to have some continuity to these signs, so spectators will recognize them easily. There should be enough signs to create a virtual roadmap of the site facilities and locations.

You may choose to have some large locator boards in prominent places showing the overall site and calling out where the viewer is at that location. This will help with the orientation of the site in general.

There will also be informational signs identifying the names of the trailers, tents, restroom facilities, vendor compounds as well as special rooms in the clubhouse. There will be credential boards that will show allowed access at that particular point as well as other special access locations.

The size of each sign will be determined based upon the location, the amount of written text per sign and the distance from which you would like the sign to be readable. The color theme of the event might be carried through in the sign program, but the use of logos on the signs is discouraged as they will become souvenir items and you may find yourself replacing a great many of signs as the event progresses.

Most of the signs are on posts buried in the ground depending on the location; others may be free standing and some will be drilled into trailers or buildings. The cost of the signs is generally based upon the square foot and the difficulty of design. You may want to do something special for the corporate identification signs in the villages since they are paying a large sum to participate. This is entirely up to you, and the corporate sales manager.

Off-site signs are generally directional signs or of the informational variety. Since the spectators need to find the parking lots, it is a good idea to have signs directing them to the different locations either by lot numbers or letters. These signs are typically much larger as vehicles have the tendency of moving fast and they will probably only be able to glance at the signs.

The speed at which vehicles are traveling will also dictate the number of signs to communicate information. Sometimes the state or local municipality will pick up the cost of these signs, sometimes they won't. You may also use variable message or electronic signs at key intersections or if you want to emphasize caution in certain areas.

You will need parking lot area signs denoting the different parking areas in the lot so the spectators can find their cars quickly.

Again I emphasize not using logos or the event name on the signs as they will be stolen as souvenirs.

The transportation cars for hotel shuttles as well as the courtesy cars for players will need to have some identifying sign on the doors either by contract or design to help speed up movement coming into or leaving the site.

It is a good idea to contact the city, state or county to see if they will provide variable message signs for you to use during the construction period of the site. Some of this was discussed earlier, but it is worth repeating. These signs may be used to direct big trucks to staging areas to lessen the impact of a long line of trucks on a major highway waiting to enter the site.

It will be easier to deal with directing the trucks to the proper location if they are all waiting in one area with no pressure to move them until ready.

As the event progresses, additional signs will likely be needed. It will be important to designate one person as the interface with the sign company; otherwise you may duplicate the sign order due to multiple people ordering the same thing. The sudden need to order signs is normally due to changes being made in spectator movement, to reduce bottlenecks in an area or more signs needed in the parking lots or people are missing the turn into the lot. These situations need to be rectified quickly.

Make sure during the bid process that the sign company has enough equipment on site to make the signs you need quickly.

The majority of the sign needs should be given in writing to the sign company well in advance. When they arrive on site ninety per cent of the signs should have been completed.

Plan ahead in this area; it isn't fair to bury the sign vendor with additional sign orders when you know that the crunch is coming. We have been blessed with an exceptional sign company which we have used the last 20 years. That will tell you how important it is to have someone who understands what you need and has been through the chaos before.

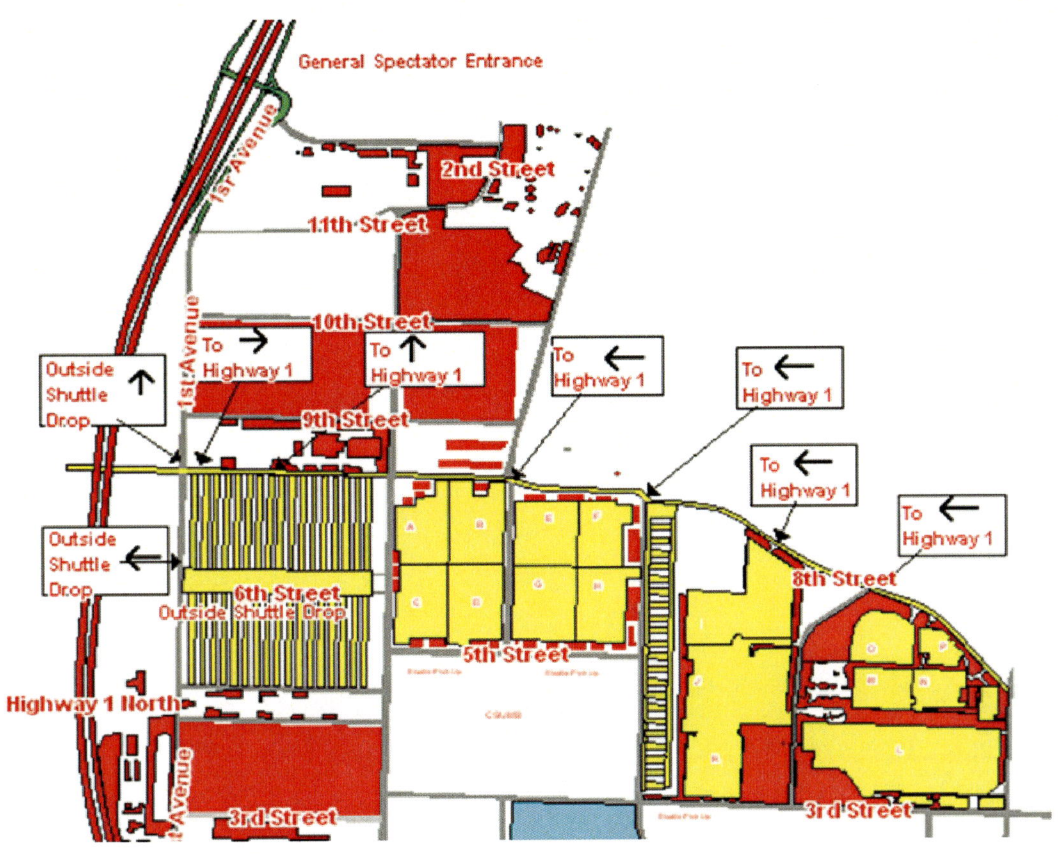

This is an example of road signs. These signs are placed along the roadways to assist the spectators in finding their way back to the main roads from the parking lots. They need to be large signs (four feet by four feet or larger) depending on the speed of the cars. The faster the cars are moving the bigger the signs need to be to be readable.

Chapter Twenty Eight

ADMISSIONS

This chapter covers a large area, since admissions is responsible for everything having to do with entering the site, special and corporate hospitality, restricted areas, vendor compounds and similar areas.

Admission credentials are broken down into three areas; tickets, badges and parking passes. Well in advance, research ticket printing companies, help design the ticket face and work with legal to come up with all the disclaimers for the venue.

Some things which might be included: the event is not responsible for acts of God, meaning the weather; refund policy, if any; disallowed items on site. This could range from the obvious like guns and knives, to cell phones, signs, chairs, banners or whatever the event deems to be unsuitable.

Determine the number of tickets to print and categorize the names on the tickets by function. The numbers are determined by the amount of people allowed on the site per day and then the number of tickets allocated to the corporate clients. You already know these numbers based upon the number of tents during the site review and facility placement.

However, you may have to increase the expected ticket number if you need to take care of special people such as government officials, special VIPs, and other event colleagues. You may further break down the ticket numbers by the allocations to the corporate table tent as well as an upgraded ticket for a food and beverage.

Once the numbers and types of tickets have been determined, be cognizant of the size of the ticket and if it is supposed to hang from the person's neck or belt. The size needs to be large enough to display the routes to the specific parking lot associated with the ticket.

The general spectator has one ticket with the route to the general spectator lot; the corporate client may have a different route to their designated lot which needs to appear on the reverse side of this ticket.

So far, the ticket size and maps to designated parking areas have been addressed. Space should be allocated the event disclaimer which includes items not permitted on site; rain and refund policies and general information the spectator should know and adhere to.

The next step is the design of the ticket face. Some printing companies can assist you. Try to stay away from photographs, if possible, as you have to obtain releases if they are copyright protected. Determine whether the ticket will be good for the entire event or if daily tickets corresponding to each day of the event will be created.

After these factors have been weighed, it's time to print. All of the tickets and badges should be numbered for control and to minimize duplication.

During the printing process it to have is advisable to have some mechanism which makes your ticket unique and difficult to reproduce. These qualities add cost to the ticket but insure no one will be reproducing your tickets. Do not want to distribute the tickets too early prior to the event in order to cut down on the time someone may have to try to copy the tickets.

There are been cases of photocopied tickets created by a sophisticated copier being distributed. Due to the ticket security measures taken, the tickets were confiscated at the admission gates. Inside the ticket brochure pocket which holds the tickets, another opportunity exists to communicate information concerning the event, whether it is about rain delays, site layout or a general summary.

At large venues it may be cost-effective to retain a company which has capabilities to print badges on site once the bulk of the badges have been pre-printed. If it is not possible for you to have a vendor on site, over-order the badge categories and quantities. In addition, create a generic badge for the late comers.

Parking passes will be a nightmare unless the numbers distributed are restricted. Space is usually very limited at any given site and the numbers allocated to each lot should not exceed what can actually be parked in the lot.

You don't want to find out what happens if there are too many parking passes and not enough space. These poor people will be circling the lots creating more congestion on the roads trying to find a place to park. And, most assuredly, they will become very irritated and will voice their displeasure.

Invariably it will be a person from the media who will write a "nice" article about the operation.

Admission gates are simply what the name implies. These "gates" are dispersed around the site at easily accessible locations for spectator entry. There might be some special gates created for specific corporate clients or vendors, located away from the general public gates or there may be special ticket lines for these people to enter quickly (an express line if you will).

The size of the gate will be determined by the space available and the volume of people expected through that particular location. You can't expect 2000 people to enter single file through an admission gate, so you need to develop four or five lines or chutes through which people can enter haves ticket checked and move on through.

The number of admission gates will change after you look at the map for the first time as you work through everything necessary. It may be caused by having residents from the surrounding area enter from two or three locations as opposed to one or a taxi/limo drop off location.

We have had as many as 22 admission gates.

This is a good time to discuss bar coding of tickets and badges. If you want to

track the number of people coming through different gates, the arrival times, total attendance per hour and have the ability to deactivate specific tickets or badges, then bar coding is a good system to employ.

The bar codes are imprinted on the tickets and badges and are programmed for access to certain areas. It is necessary to have scanning machines to read the bar codes. These machines require low voltage power at all the locations used. Scanning will slow down the admissions process a bit so you may have to expand the number of gates. The system is not inexpensive, but if control and accountability are requirements, this is a good system.

In addition to the people who are scanning the tickets, it would be wise to have some security personnel in these locations to deal with tickets which have been turned off, or any scalpers who may be in the area.

Admissions personnel may need phone access at the locations to verify information or to transmit data back to the central processing location. The central processing center is called Will Call. All of the tickets which have been sold appear on databases so they can be looked up and verified quickly. People have the ability to leave tickets at this location for others who will pick them up later in the day or later in the week.

You may find that due to site limitations that it may be necessary to have more than one Will Call location.

If this is the case, the communication between the Will Call trailers needs to be seamless.

Databases need to be accessed at each location through a network for verification. If this system breaks down, you will experience long lines and many frustrated people.

Will Call offices will most likely need radios to communicate with the other admission areas for potential problems. This would require some golf carts to travel the site to different locations should problems arise or to check on how the system is working.

It is an ever-changing animal, as during different times of the day the gates may be utilized more heavily than at other times. Plan to make adjustments as the event progresses.

Chapter Twenty Nine

TELEVISION NETWORKS

It's desirable to have an event televised by a major network due to the revenues received by the event. There are numerous networks to choose from and, depending upon the event and its drawing power, an arrangement with a network might be established. Typically, sports cable channels, one of the major networks and possibly some foreign networks all want access to the event. If you have a smaller event, it may be necessary for you to pay for the television coverage which would involve selling all of the advertising spots necessary for the televised coverage. Research this carefully, as it is likely that your event may only be able to afford one of the lesser known networks for your coverage.

If this is the case, then particular attention should be given to the networks' compound space requirements and other needs. Requirements can vary anywhere from 50,000 square feet up to 120,000 square feet depending upon whether network personnel will be able to park cars in the compound. The area will be secured by a chain link fence to keep unwanted guests away. Depending upon the location of the compound, the fence may require windscreen for aesthetic purposes.

Work with the networks once the compound location is decided as to the type of ground in the compound. Typically, it would be a combination of crushed rock and grass. The production trucks would park on the rock due to their weight and everything else would be on the grass. In the event of rain, rock may help avoid this location from becoming a quagmire.

Communications requirements need to be discussed early so that the cabling can be accomplished simultaneously to other wiring to help reduce the expense. At the same time the television feed from the broadcast partner needs to be received in the compound as the networks want to see how the event is broadcasting. The scoring operation will also be run to this area for various updates during the broadcast.

Potable water will need to be brought to the site for the network's catering operation. Add this to the list of topics to discuss the health department. If water is not readily available, chlorinated water tanks may be allowed. In some locations you may be able to sink wells but each location is different and you have to check with the appropriate agency.

The appropriate number of badges and parking passes will need to be produced for the network to gain access to the site as well as parking passes. Parking for staff is very important and the numbers could top 250 vehicles. If there are not enough parking spaces available within the compound, a parking lot proximate will be preferred. Shuttles will run from the lot to the compound at their expense. It is much more efficient for overall operation if enough parking is available in the compound.

Having worked out the compound space allocated to the various networks, an onsite survey needs to be conducted for placement of camera and announce towers. The announce towers have also been discussed in Chapter Twenty two. It will be important to have someone familiar with the rules to be present in case the placement of the towers could potentially interfere with play. If this becomes an issue, generally a compromise is reached.

During this survey the superintendent will become aware of any trees which may need to be trimmed to assist with the placement of towers and platforms.

Additional trimming may be necessary once the cameras are in place holes are viewed through the lens. There may be other locations where cameras will be located, all of which need to be approved by you or someone designated for that purpose. In addition to announce positions, there may be some locations where networks may desire to have sets built for interviews of different people during the event. Typically the clubhouse or another part of the site or signature hole appears in the background. You will find that available space on the site is shrinking quickly. Be open-minded and creative to meet these requests as broadcast coverage reaches the masses. In the event of rain it will often be necessary to provide protected areas to conduct player or official interviews during the delay.

It is helpful to provide the networks with the event vendor list so they might use the same vendors and get preferred pricing. The vendors like the extra business and it provides some continuity to the event.

In addition to the major networks, local affiliates of the major networks will need to be accommodated. This equipment typically is a van with booms which rise during the broadcast to accept signals. Of course, every television crew wants to be set up in a prime location, but this isn't possible. Affiliates may be located by the driving range but in some extremes, the locations might face a non-active fairway. It is really out of necessity, not design, that these locations are pressed into service. You have to fit everything else and then see what's remaining. Prioritize

One note about the local broadcast affiliates: make sure that their microwave signal does not interfere with the major network coverage.

Be aware that you are normally dealing with the head of production and not the personnel actually laying the cable. From time to time, the cable installation becomes a frenzied and unwieldy process. Designate a person to oversee the networks during installation time or you will be spending a lot of time trying to explain why areas were trampled or destroyed. Communication with the production manager will help alleviate these problems.

Generators will be set around the tower locations which will require servicing. Consult with the vendor as to the location and route to take. When the announce towers are constructed, room will be needed for air conditioning units and restroom facilities. These areas are normally fenced once the construction is completed in order to keep unauthorized people out of the area. A firm discussion with the networks needs to occur concerning golf cart usage.

Photo provided by T&B Equipment

It is imperative that personnel understand where they are allowed to park around the towers and what proper etiquette entails.

Unless you are specific, golf carts will be parked all over the site, mostly in the areas they aren't supposed to be and normally in your way. You will solve a lot of problems by discussing this in advance.

The networks are very self-sufficient and will usually only approach you when they need help with access to an area or require some tree trimming. I have found few problems with any of the networks I have worked with over the years.

This is an example of a single camera tower the networks would erect for the television coverage.

This is an example of a four-booth television announce tower. Notice how the air conditioning for the booths is tucked underneath the structure. There is also a single portopot for the broadcasters located adjacent to the booths. This structure takes a great deal of space. The bleacher company did an excellent job fitting this structure in such a confined area.

Photo provided by T&B Equipment

Chapter Thirty

SCHEDULE

Back into the schedule or timeline based upon when the event is supposed to start.

Once the facilities are placed on the map and major vendors selected, installation of temporary roads and communications cable can start well in advance of the event.

The vendor who will set the pace will be the décor and tent vendor. They will need to work backwards based upon the completion deadlines of corporate tents. If the tent vendor can keep the pace, then life is good. Everyone follows the tent vendor. The tents need to be complete with side wall and ceiling liners. Tent installation is followed by the air conditioning and subsequently by electrical vendors who begin in the completed tents.

There will be times the tent vendor is ahead of schedule so it would be wise to have thought about other areas where they can move to keep them ahead of schedule.

During this time the floors are marked in exact locations for power outlets, television and phone cable locations. Then the carpet is laid in the tent. The carpet is cut in the prescribed locations and the cables are pulled through.

Once all of these things have been accomplished, the décor company comes in and adds the upgrades the client has ordered. This could be as little as a built-in bar or as large as hard wall constructed around the entire interior of the tent. The types and levels of upgrades are too numerous to mention.

When the décor has been completed, then the landscaping is placed around the tent and the tables and chairs are placed inside. The televisions and phone sets are added at this time. The caterer then takes over and sets up the food prep tent areas with refrigerated coolers, ice merchandisers, work tables, buffets and table linen. You are now ready to go.

Now this sounds simple and in a perfect world it would be, but there are thousands of things that can go wrong and hundreds of things that do. Trucks don't show up on time so certain things cannot be accomplished; rain causes delays because the site can't be accessed due to the ground being too soft. Tents have an infestation of a rare variety of the gypsy moth. All these things eat up the schedule. When you started the day you were ahead by two days and by the time the day finished, you were three days behind. It can happen that quickly.

The bad list can go on and on, but it's critical to be able to adapt to the problems as they occur. If you can't work in one area, go to another. All the work has to be done, so try to keep moving.

It is the goal to finish two days prior to the event. The corporate tents need to be completed this far in advance for corporate tent services to have a walk through with the corporate clients. They will work closely with the décor company to make sure the tents they need to inspect have been completed. This time is also spent

checking all the amenities offered to each client.

These items include checking all the phone lines for the correct phone numbers, making sure the lines are active, and checking the cable feeds to the televisions. A client would not be very happy if his television didn't work. They also check to make sure that all of the electrical equipment is plugged into the correct outlet so breakers don't start popping and that the air conditioning units are functioning properly. There will always be things that will threaten your ability to finish on time.

Some equipment will be delivered at the last minute primarily to affect cost savings. This, however, will cause other things to be put on hold until the first thing is in. For example, parking lots may not close until later than expected, delaying the time to place bike rack fencing.

There are a lot of things out of your control, so make the best of things you can control.

In weekly onsite vendor meetings, construction projects for that week are discussed and adjustments made. Communicate with vendors about how the schedule is progressing. You will gain a feel as to whether you are on pace to meet the schedule or not. It may be necessary for the vendors to increase the work force in certain areas to keep pace.

Communicate to the vendors.

If there is trouble due to another vendor is slowing them down, find a way to speed up that vendor.

Because all vendors are under a great deal of stress, yelling at them will really not help the cause! Make it abundantly clear you not happy with the progress and expect immediate improvement. You have to find your own style of motivating your vendors without alienating them or creating a worse situation.

Following the event, you will need to have a tear down schedule. This should be discussed with the vendors during a meeting to be held during event week when things have calmed down and the event is underway running smoothly. Convey to them the areas the club would like to have returned to normal operations first and determine a schedule. As long as everyone knows what to expect, the post event chaos will be reduced.

In the back of the book, I have included a timeline for an event to be held in June of any year.

Chapter Thirty One

VOLUNTEERS & WELLNESS TEAM

Volunteers are the backbone of any event.

This is worth repeating: Volunteers are the backbone of any event.

No event that I know of could exist without the dedication of the volunteer force. Each event possesses different volunteer needs; some might require 50, others 5000. It just depends upon the size of the event.

If your event is large, people will want to be involved and will most likely contact you. If it is small you may have to rely on the club, area golf or tennis organizations, club professionals or outbound mailings.

Whatever the method, it is imperative to a smooth operating event to get volunteers needed to facilitate operations.

The first thing to do, besides setting up an office, is to outline the job duties and create a job description for each. It would be wise to select a chairman for each committee so some of the workload can be passed to the chairman. Develop schedules of shifts that each volunteer will be working and the criteria for developing the shifts to be worked by the volunteers.

This varies greatly. Some shifts may only be four hours; others may be longer depending upon the position. One benefit to volunteers is when they aren't working they have a chance to see the event.

Normally a uniform is provided to volunteers at a minimal cost, and meals are served for volunteers working that day.

Depending on the availability of close proximity parking, it may be offered to volunteers to sweeten the deal, or even a small gift provided to show your appreciation.

Make no mistake; volunteers are very important to any event.

As the start of the event gets closer, there will be training sessions to teach the volunteers their assigned tasks. Security back-ground checks may need to be performed if volunteers are driving vehicles.

The first day of any event is called "Black Monday". It is so named because the first day tends to have a lot of confusion... where the volunteers are supposed to report, their tasks, volunteer no-shows, food didn't show up on time, there is no coffee, the shuttles left without volunteers or they left their badge at home. By the second day, things are usually running pretty smoothly and by the third day, operations are really humming.

Some volunteers will be carrying radios for communication and this area requires training. Most think of radios as telephones, not realizing that no one else can talk as long as that little button is pushed in.

Most volunteer chairman will have cell phones to receive quick communication as the need arises.

The Wellness Team consists of various health care providers including doctors of Chiropractic, massage therapists, athletic trainers, physical therapists and hyperbaric chamber technicians.

In some instances, endermologists and acupuncturists have also been included. Several administrative assistants will normally be recruited to assist with the required paperwork.

This team was designed to accommodate the physical stresses experienced by volunteers, players, caddies and event staff during the event marathon.

It was realized years ago that this level of treatment was well received and created a more relaxing environment.

Since this event changes location each year, it creates its own set of challenges. The location of the caddie and volunteer hospitality, geography and access to the site, will affect its operation during the week.

Some locations are not user friendly, meaning the player's and caddie's access is not easily accessible. Other times it will be adjacent to the range or other player areas.

In addition, state and local governmental rules and regulations along with event requirements, will dictate how the Wellness Team conducts their operation. It will be important that the Wellness Tem chairperson is in contact with the state and/or local governing boards for each health care discipline.

This should take place before recruitment begins.

The Wellness Team chairperson should be informed as much as practical to avoid recruiting someone who may be disqualified later in the process. The sooner accurate information is received will, in the long run, save time, effort and resources.

The recruitment process for the usually begins in October for the event that will take place the following June. Each potential team member is required to fill out an application with passport photos included. An extensive interview is conducted, either face to face or over the phone.

All applicants and team members must also submit to a background check as required by anyone interacting with the players. Recruitment usually concludes in December.

Any potential team members applying after the normal recruitment period ends will be waitlisted.

At that point, each health care provider is sent a Policies and Procedure manual, which they are strongly encouraged to read. The manual explains to health care team members what is expected from them prior to, during and after the Championship.

There are two points that should be emphasized about the recruitment process. First, contacting and communicating with the state and/or local governing boards for each health care discipline.

Informing the appropriate agencies of the creation of the Wellness Team and complying with state and local laws and regulations will always will be a priority.

Even though the Wellness Team is created for only one calendar week and is usually set up in a temporary structure, it should still be run like a traditional health care facility. Second, the recruitment of health care providers from the general geographic vicinity of each venue is encourages.

It enhances the "local flavor" that will please the local government as well as event officials. Communications is maintained by the Wellness Team chairperson with all team members, from the conclusion of recruitment in December until the event the following June.

Usually this is done through a series of emails. Team members are required to respond to each email for several reasons. It lets the chairperson know that the email was received, that it was understood and that the team member is still committed to volunteering at the event.

Scheduling of the Wellness Team shifts usually takes place at the beginning of April (two months before the event). By this time, the chairperson will know the location and dimensions of the Caddie Hospitality and Volunteer Hospitality tents.

The dimensions of each tent will determine the amount of space that will be allotted to the Wellness Team. The chairperson, with guidance from event staff will determine the number of stations needed to be manned within that space.

Each team member is requested to work, at a minimum, two 5-hour shifts. The scheduling of up to 100 Wellness Team members is a process that can be both frustrating and rewarding.

The chairperson will try to maintain a balance between manpower requirements and team member availability. It will not always work out as hoped or planned.

The chairperson recognizes that the team members are volunteers and that the intent is to make everyone's overall experience at the event a positive one.

Equipment needed by the Wellness Team is usually delivered to the venue approximately two months before the event. All equipment will be removed

within one week of the event's conclusion. A sign order is also placed two months before the event. The signs indicate the types of treatment available and hours of operation. Signs will be strategically placed for maximum exposure.

Caddies, Players, event staff and other support staff are offered treatments at the Caddie Hospitality Tent. Types of treatments available are Chiropractic, massage therapy and hyperbaric chamber therapy. In addition, athletic trainers, physical therapists, acupuncturists and endermologists may be available.

Anyone being treated in the Caddie Hospitality tent must fill out a medical history form and sign a consent form.

Volunteers, who are working shifts for that particular day, are offered a chair massage at the Volunteer Hospitality tent. Volunteers being treated must also sign a consent form.

Within a week of the event, there will be a volunteer training session for all Wellness Team members. The session is conducted by event staff with additional information added by the Wellness Team chairperson.

Each team member receives a volunteer packet that includes their personal credential, a parking permit, food vouchers and a volunteer handbook.

Each item in the packet is explained along with other pertinent general event information such as parking location and hours, where the food vouchers are valid etc.

Each member also receives a Wellness Team uniform golf shirt that they are required to wear during their assigned shift.

Chapter Thirty Two

STAFFING

If your event is large, there will be many moving parts and there should be a hierarchy with the Tournament Director at the helm, to manage operations. The Tournament Director will normally answer to a Board of Directors or some other group. On a lateral line underneath the Tournament Director should be legal, admissions, Volunteer coordinator, operations, corporate/marketing, accounting and insurance. Naturally under each category would be other key figures with specific duties pertaining to the job function assigned.

Legal would be responsible for the production and review of all contracts based upon the scope of work to be provided by each vendor. Make sure each area provides legal with enough lead time to review each contract; otherwise they will be trying to finish contracts just weeks prior to the event.

Admissions are responsible for the production and distribution of all tickets, badges and parking passes. It is, however, a group effort when it comes to the access allowed by each badge. For example, one vendor may be allowed into the clubhouse to respond to necessary repairs and maintenance of equipment and other vendors may not have that same access. This is because the second vendor had no reason to be in the clubhouse. This is the reason for badge access. Badges have been known to number in the thousands, depending upon the support needed for the event. This process is structured to limit those who do not need access to the property. If there is a bona fide need for any emergency repair, the company responding may be met at the access gate and then escorted to the problem area. If your event is in high demand, one which will draw a large attendance, you may be overwhelmed by requests.

The Volunteer Coordinator has been discussed in a previous chapter, but this person is responsible for recruiting and training all volunteers. This area can be daunting and the number of staff in this area will continue to rise as you close in on the actual event. Normally this operation will begin two years prior to the event itself to allow time for recruitment. This department will also act as liaison to the needs of the players, and will interact with all the other groups to accomplish that goal. It might include player vehicles, player transportation, player registration as well as player and VIP housing.

Corporate/Marketing is responsible for working with the Championship Director and Operations in determining the size and location of the corporate chalets on the site. This would include the amenities offered with each package. Normally that package would consist of a standard tent, which is up-gradable, a specified number of tickets, also up-gradable, update sessions to distribute information, preferred parking areas, and a specific number of golf outings.

Once these things have been determined and priced, this department sells the packages to prospective clients with hopes of selling the complete inventory. This process begins two to three years prior to the event. As the event begins construction, this department insures that what has been promised is delivered within the time specified. It doesn't end there. During the event, corporate

hospitality services insure the needs of the corporate clients are met and that their experience is good enough to have them sign up for many years to come.

Accounting's function is to keep track of all the money generated and spent, focusing on the budget and acting as the watch dog of the event. If you are under budget, they want to know why; if you are over budget, they really want to know why.

However, if you have done your homework, you will usually be close to budget. Expect surprises... they always arise. If you try to squeeze the budget, and not include enough money to handle unforeseeable problems then you will over spend in some areas. You can only hope you are under in other areas to compensate.

Keep accounting abreast of all changes as they occur.

Insurance is usually outsourced and covers items such as rental trucks, golf carts, and other rental equipment, including office trailers. If accidents occur, accounting and the insurance company need to be notified immediately. Prepare written statements of what has transpired, as well as a police report if needed.

If your event is on a beautiful golf course with rolling hills, someone is likely to fall down and sue you. Get used to it, it will happen. All you can do is ensure all facilities are constructed to building codes and there is no negligence on your part.

Administrative covers all the other people behind-the- scenes. It may include support staff for each of the departments discussed or it may include the support staff of the tournament director. Normally any person involved who is paid by the event will be considered an administrative cost.

Other costs would include travel, office supplies, car rentals, supplies and other administrative needs. These costs have a tendency to get out of hand if not watched carefully.

Operations are responsible for almost all of the chapters in this book. At the very least, operations will touch every area previously discussed. Depending on the size of the event, the operation staff starts out relatively small, probably only two or three people, as most of the work 12 months out is talking to potential vendors. If the event stays in the same place every year, then the staff will be somewhat predictable.

Also, if you use the same vendors year after year then the job becomes a little easier. However, if the site moves every year, then you will likely have new vendors in most areas. If you have signed multi-year deals with major vendors, it is imperative to get them to the new site to review the construction plans.

Due to the stress of moving every year, training programs for entry-level personnel should be on-going to replace those who may depart. It is not an easy life on the road, so cross-training is key.

Five months out, arrange a few interns to assist you and your staff as the remaining months begins to close in. The responsibilities may include the signage and banner programs, as well as day-to-day issues which would allow you to

concentrate on other areas.

One key area for an intern will be to assume responsibility for all of the keys for the site. This would include trailers, golf carts, heavy equipment, pickup trucks, and any padlocks for entry/exit.

I could dedicate a whole chapter to the topic of keys. The person put in charge of keys must be very detail oriented. A master key board needs to be created with all the keys numbered; you may have different boards for each operational group.

Trailer keys are a nightmare, especially since there may be in excess of 90 trailers. Three keys need to be made for every lock; you may cut this down by telling the people to use one door as an entry which will save time and money.

Dedicate one person, maybe more, to handle the trailer keys. This area will need access by the TV crew, cabling crews, phone, furniture, bottled water and possibly fax and copier provider. The trailers should remain unlocked until items of value are placed in them.

Always have backup keys to the forklifts, bobcats and other equipment as well as the pickup trucks.

To alleviate the key problem with keyed locks for the gates, you may want to use combination locks. Make sure the appropriate people know the combinations, such as the superintendent who tends to get upset if he can't get on his course. Be careful with the combinations, as someone is liable to ask on the radio while others are listening for the combination to a lock.

Whoever you assign to this responsibility will need to understand that they and their assistants will be running prior to the event, trying to stay ahead of all the vendors who need access.

An administrative assistant will be responsible for scheduling vendor meetings, preparing agendas and will be well-versed in answering basic questions about the site. Make sure this person has a script of what to say about various topics. You would not want them saying a parking area is close to the site or that certain buses run very fifteen minutes, if it isn't true.

So help them out, by writing down what they can and cannot say. Messages may be taken if answers are not readily known. The administrative support person will also be responsible for keeping updated files and distributing information to all concerned.

Two months out from the event, begin to pick up outside operations staff, normally four to six people. They will be joined by four more the six weeks out. This core group and specific vendors are responsible for all that happens on site during setup, and throughout the event. They will be responsible for placing miles of wind screen on fence, painting portolet enclosures, and directing various deliveries to correct locations. They unlock trailers, deliver packages, unload golf carts, construct and reconstruct items as necessary.

After all, operations have touched every area.

During this time operations is only as good as its staff. I have been blessed with many years of great crews and a few years of not so great crews. Supervision is always the key. With strong supervision everything else will follow.

If an operations crew is going to accomplish their jobs well, they need to have the correct tools. Have assorted tools ready when they arrive to work, researched by the interns months in advance. Circular saws, drills, hammers, snips, duct tape, and much more should have been stocked in the operations trailer ready to go. You have purchased first aid kits and published directions to the nearest hospital for all staff and all vendors. Time sheets should be filled out by the operations staff and submitted weekly to payroll.

Make sure staff has adequate rain gear. A sick employee doesn't help during crunch time.

The operations people should know the drill; most of them have come from other events. They know about the 16-18 hour days, the problems with rain, and the unreasonable demands sometimes bestowed on them.

But this is what they do. There is a great deal of pride when the event is over and deemed a success.

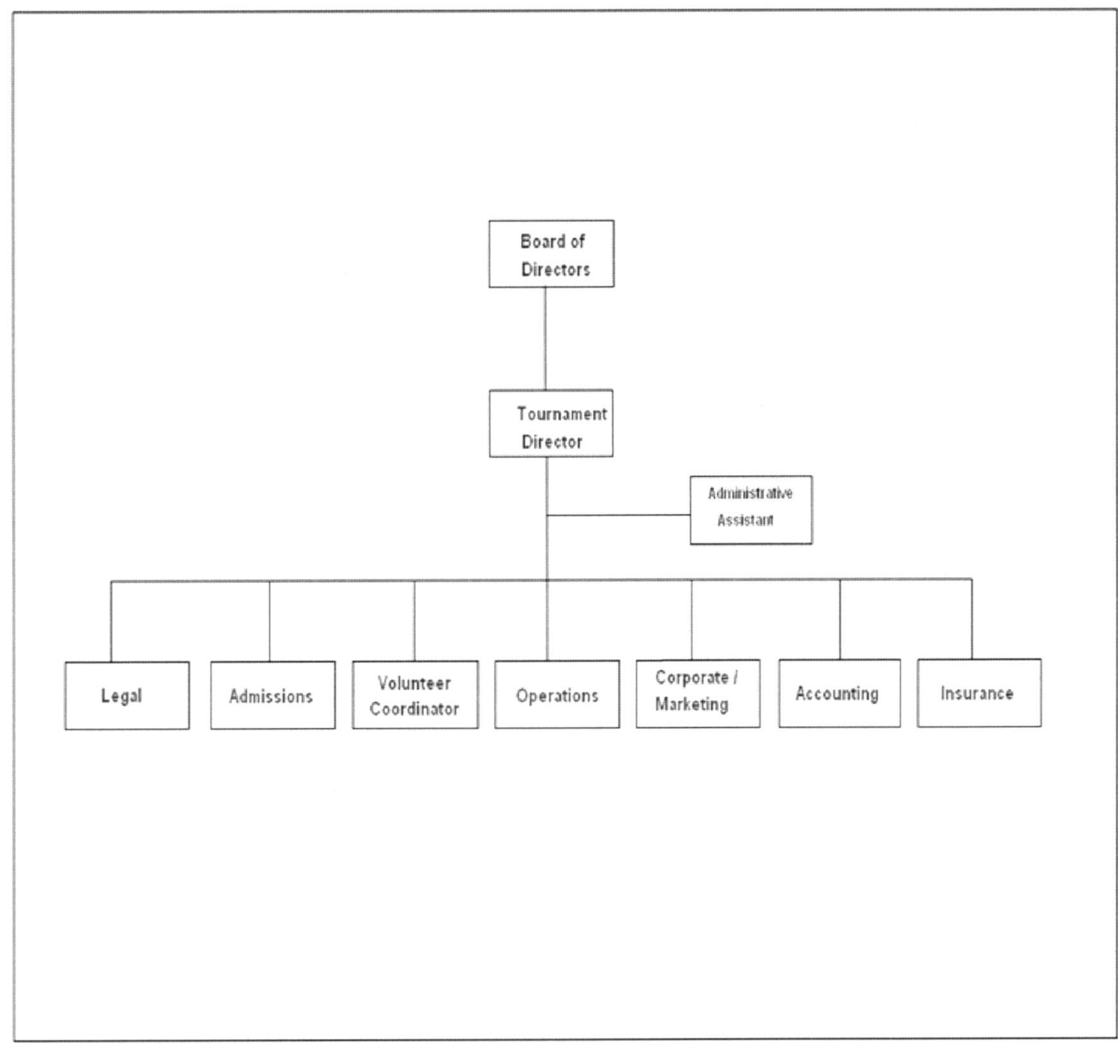

The above represents a typical organization chart for an event.

Chapter Thirty Three

CLUB HARMONY

It doesn't matter whether your event is being held at a tennis club or a golf country club. Things need to be communicated to maintain harmony. And even after they are communicated, you will need to demonstrate a great deal of patience in getting your point across.

Most clubs are going to want to know what you are doing or what is planned so they can keep the membership informed.

The contract with the club may clearly state that you have full run of the site and are responsible for the damage, but make no mistake, they still expect to be kept in the loop. Club officials may want you to begin bleacher construction on a certain hole and to save the clubhouse bleachers until last. There is no problem with this, but some things tend to get lost in the shuffle.

An agreed timeline of installation would be helpful for both parties.

The superintendent may want to know the routes communicated to vendors to get around the course so he can protect the grass. He may or may not be concerned about the trees which need to come down or be trimmed, but regardless, it is a good idea to work well with the superintendent.

Remember, you and the event are invading his area, and you are going to need his assistance. He is your first line of defense with the club.

It will be helpful if the club and/or the superintendent have been involved with events before, as they will know what to expect. It needs to be recognized that no matter how careful you are during the set-up of the event, the site in all likelihood will be heavily disrupted during the event.

It will be restored, but if expectations are managed, stress levels will be reduced.

Even though the contract may be specific, there are generally gray areas which need to be reckoned with. It is a give and take situation, one that requires both sides to use common sense with the understanding that each one is striving for the same goal: the best event possible.

In some cases the membership feels that they are in a better position to know what works best at their club as they may have had different events over the years. It will take time and patience for them to see the wisdom of why you are doing things the way you are.

In most cases, they will come around and at least understand "why".

Sometimes you may find yourself being flexible towards the club's desires because in the big picture, it will not impact the final plan. It is important to be a good partner.

Rain during setup may cause many problems. Roads have been built to assist the

heavy equipment during rain, but you can't build roads everywhere.

Rain and heavy equipment will create mud in grass very quickly so to be prepared to work in areas which will cause the least damage.

There will be times that it will difficult to achieve, especially if the rain hits a few days prior to the event. As the amount of time left comes down to the wire, finishing touches need to take place.

During this time, the superintendent will need to set priorities and provide guidance.

Hopefully when it is all said and done the event and the club has both achieved what they set out to do...stage a wonderful event where the membership and operations team were pleased with the outcome. the event is over, be as careful as when you started. Vendors need to stay on the roads and adhere to specified routing.

Some misplaced heavy equipment causing ruts on grass can negate all the goodwill achieved during setup.

The club will appreciate a timeline for the tear down of the event. Again, you may be asked to remove the facilities around the clubhouse first to get back to some normalcy. Devise a timeline that works for all parties involved. After all, it was a group effort during setup and should be during tear down.

Just know that there will always be rough spots, but invariably there will be people at the club who will understand the goals and will assist toward that end.

Chapter Thirty Four

RESTORATION

Within any contract will be a clause about site restoration. Most contracts are written with the intent that your organization has use of the entire site, but are responsible for any wear and tear on the facility beyond what is reasonable.

This restoration needs to be approached in a fair and reasonable fashion. There are obvious areas of restoration, such as temporary roads. The roads will have to be removed and top soil brought in to bring the area back up to grade, ready for seed.

But there are things which might fall into gray areas, including the cost for removing trees where the bleachers were to be placed around the greens. If this was not included in the initial contract, it would need to be worked out.

If the corporate villages are placed on tennis courts the courts may need resurfacing and the fence reinstalled. Any asphalt that has broken up due to the set up and tear down of the event will have to be repaired, however, if the asphalt was already cracked and breaking up in places, the event should not be responsible for the entire repair.

The surface conditions should be documented in writing and photographically before the installation. These costs will need to be priced and agreed to by the club or venue prior to the event so there are no disputes after the event.

If the club plans to redo the tennis facility, they may want the money allocated for the repair instead of repairing the tennis courts.

There may be areas of the course where heavy equipment has caused ruts in the ground. These areas need to be smoothed out and reseeded. Fence pipe driven through irrigation pipe during installation would have to be fixed.

All electrical or phone lines that were disconnected to allow the tournament system to be installed would need to be reconnected.

If the corporate tents were constructed on fairways, this would have to be discussed.

Normally, you would not be responsible for the dead grass created under these tents by the lack of sunlight for such a long period of time. The club would have realized this was going to happen prior to the signing of the contract for the event.

If your event is one which moves every year, the club might send representatives to a prior event to see the magnitude and scope of work involved. This would definitely be advisable so there are no surprises.

There may have been the need to remove trees from certain areas beyond what may have been spelled out in the contract. Replacement trees may need to be

purchased in those incidences.

Beyond what has been discussed, there are always things you or the event site will disagree on and which will need to be negotiated to an amicable settlement.

In all probability, the event was a success and the host site will want to host it again so it would behoove both parties to come to some kind of agreement and move on.

Chapter Thirty Five

TIME TO GO

This is probably my favorite chapter. The event is over and, in all likelihood, it was a huge success. Sadly, you probably have almost as much work now as you did while setting up. As they say, the party is over and it's time to go.

Some actions need to happen right as the last ball is being hit. Security needs to tighten up concerning the things which will tend to get stolen. Your crew is out taking down the flags and banners before they become souvenir items.

After the banners and flags have been secured, you want your crew to get some rest. Make sure all the villages are secure and any area which may have a television, copier or fax is locked up; then cut your crew loose for the evening. By this time it will usually be around 9:00 pm.

Check the shuttles to insure they are running smoothly, and discuss with dispatch a specific time to shut it down later in the evening. Once the celebration party has ended and all of the spectators are gone from the site, its business as usual for the overnight security.

The next day, concentrate the television distribution crew on retrieving all the televisions from all areas. While they are accomplishing that daunting task, have another crew working with the copier company retrieving all of the copiers and faxes. Still another crew is working with the bottled water company picking up all of the water dispensers from all the locations.

The day after any event is like a free for all. There are many truck and vendors trying to occupy the same space to pick up equipment. It is semi-organized chaos.

After the likely theft items have been retrieved, have some of your crew direct trucks to the proper locations for equipment pick up. The soft drink company has huge box trucks in the village removing refrigerator coolers; the décor company, which had worked into the previous night, has returned to strip the interiors of the tent. There are three dumpsters on each side of every village, moved into location in the early morning to provide the décor vendor a place to discard the broken-down interiors.

There will be drivers hauling dumpsters continuously throughout the day trying to keep up with the demolition of the interior of the tents. The décor company has another job waiting in another city, so they are in a hurry. The tent vendor is removing all of the furniture from the tents behind the décor vendor.

During this time the electrical and HVAC vendors have disconnected the electrical from the generators and the HVAC units. The generator company has a huge fork lift and is moving the generators to a staging area.

At the same time ecology crews are removing trash from the course and from each tent, following the décor company. If trash is not out of the tents before tear down, there will be trash all over the site. This would not be pretty.

Each vendor has a plan because a meeting is held right before the end of the event to designate the hot spot areas which need to be broken down first. This schedule is created, based upon a reopening schedule the club may have for certain areas. Or, vendors who need to ship equipment to another site may request early priority in breaking down their materials.

Each vendor is working in concert with the others, not stepping on toes. There is a lot to remove and a shortage of space, but as far as you are concerned the pressure is off. While the club attempts to hurry you along, officials knew and approved the removal schedule long before the event.

The caterer has already removed everything from the villages and there are trucks in this compound removing the kitchen equipment. They'll be done and gone by the weekend following the event; one down and seven to go. The concessionaire will be next. Once the equipment is off the course and back in the staging compound, focus is on the soft drink company, ice company and propane company to pick up equipment.

Each vendor conducts a walk-through with you before they can leave as you are not to be stuck trying to chase down vendor subcontractors for the pick-up of their equipment.

The décor company is finished and ready to leave. The site looks good so they depart. Remaining are tents, electrical, HVAC and bleachers, which will be the last to leave. There are many, many trucks to load.

Your crews will be assigned to pick up or supervise the loading of all the bike rack on trucks to return the racks to the rental company. Make sure that all the furniture you ordered has been picked up and removed from all the trailers. The enclosures around the portable toilets need to come down so the company can access the units.

Get everything off the course, especially from areas which don't have roads, before any possible rain hits.

Once that is done, breathe a little easier.

By now hopefully enough has been cleared around the clubhouse so this area may be reopened. You know that it will still be dangerous for cars and fork lifts to be occupying the same area, so you tell everyone to slow down and be careful.

The DOT has been asked to bring back the variable message signs to alert traffic that the area is a construction zone again.

The trailer company has begun to remove the office trailers. Remind them that there is limited time to get the trailers off site, because additional space is needed to load trucks. It took over 250 trucks on the install and it will take at least that many on the way out. It may take more trucks depending upon the additional supplies purchased prior and during the event.

Once all the trailers are gone, the tents are broken down and removed to the compound. There is nothing left on course but the temporary roads which have been built. The bleachers are still coming down and this process will continue for,

at least another week.

Begin removing the rock roads and stockpiling the rock at a predetermined place on the site for future use by the superintendent. If the rock is not to remain on site, the rock vendor will have made arrangements as to where the rock will be delivered upon removal.

The operations crew has dwindled down to a few remaining people who supervise the temps removing the remainder of the trash. All of the items rented or purchased need to shipped. After that, it's a waiting game for the remaining bleachers and the tent people loading trucks.

During this time you will be working on the expenses to be billed back to vendors or other people which will reduce your overall costs.

Finally... at long last... you are finished. Check with the club one last time before hitting the road to the next site. The superintendent will be aware of the electrician who will come the next day to disconnect the field office and the trailer company will pull it out to be used the next time.

Time to go.

Chapter Thirty Six

Operations Punch List

1. Place Facilities					
	A. Tents				
		1. Corporate Tents			
		2. Merchandise Tent			
		3. Support Tents			
		4. Determine Decking			
			a. Height of Decks		
			b. Surveyor		
				1. Cad drawings	
		5. Contract Tents			
			a. Partners		
			b. NBC		
		6. Décor			
			a. Company		
			b. Cost		
			c. Layout		
			d. Timeline		
			e. Equipment		
			f. Timeline for Installation		
			g. Theme		
		7. Media Tent			
			a. Size		
		8. Interview			
			a. Size		
		9. Dining			
			a. Size		
		10. Player Hospitality			
			a. Size		
		11. USGA Hospitality			
			a. Size		

		12. Member Hospitality			
			a. Size		
		13. Concessions			
			a. Size		
			b. Location		
	B. Compounds				
		1. Locations			
			a. Size		
				1. Tent	
				2. Electrical	
				3. HVAC	
				4. Décor	
				5. Networks	
				6. Bleachers	
				7. Catering	
				8. Concessions	
				9. Landscaping	
				10.Media	
		2. Phone			
		3. Timeline			
		4. Type surface			
	C. Communications				
		1. Phone			
			a. Locations		
			b. Quantity		
			c. Features(restricted)		
			d. Costs		
			e. Switchboard		
			f. Standby		
			g. Unions		
			h. Layout		
			i. Carts		
			j. Truck Parking		
			k. Networks		
			l. Payphones		
			m. Credentials		
			n. Phone Directory		
		2. Scoring			
			a. Locations		
			b. Quantity		
			c. Costs		
			d. Standby		
			e. Unions		
			f. Layout		
			g. Carts		

			h. Trucks		
			i. Parking		
			j. Credentials		
		3. Cable			
			a. Locations		
			b. Quantity		
			c. Costs		
			d. Standby		
			e. Unions		
			f. Layout		
			g. Carts		
			h. Parking		
			i. Credentials		
		4. Radios			
			a. Groups		
			b. Numbers		
			c. Cost		
			d. Repeaters		
			e. Truck Placement		
			f. Timing		
			g. Standby		
			h. Barter		
			i. Credentials		
		5. Cell Phones			
			a. Groups		
			b. Quantity		
			c. Phone Numbers		
			d. Barter		
			e. Standby		
			f. COWS		
			g. Credentials		
			h. Parking		
			i. Timing		
	D. Electrical				
		1. Shore Power			
			a. Early Installations		
			b. Available Power		
			c. Cost		
			d. Lead time		
		2. Generators			
			a. Locations		
			b. Backup Locations		
			c. Size		
			d. Tanks		
			e. Fueling		
			f. Cost		
			g. Freight		
			h. Standby		
			i. Delivery		
		3. Unions			

			a. Feasibility	
			b. Cost	
			c. Cap	
		4. Responsibilities		
			a. Supervise all Electrical	
				1. Fueling 2. Light Towers
	E. HVAC			
		1. Locations		
		2. Cost		
		3. Split Units		
		4. Size		
		5. Chillers		
		6. Placement		
		7. Timing		
		8. Other		
	F. Trailers			
		1. Locations		
		2. Size		
		3. Cost		
		4. Delivery		
		5. Use		
		6. Steps		
		7. Damage		
		8. Cleaning		
		9. Special		
			a. Fitness	
				1. Locations
				2. Power
				3. Arrival
			b. Repair Vans	
				1. Locations
				2. Power
				3. Arrival
			c. Caddie Food	
				1. Locations
				2. Power
				3. Arrival
	G. Ecology			
		1. Portopots		
			a. Locations	
			b. Numbers	
			c. Pre & Post Championship	
			d. Supplies	
				1. Towelettes
				2. Sanitizers

			e. Carts		
			f. Fencing		
			g. Dump Locations		
			h. Truck Staging		
			i. Credentials		
			j. Radios		
			k. Cell Phone		
		2. Restroom Trailers			
			a. Locations		
			b. Numbers		
			c. Cost		
			d. Design		
			e. Delivery		
			f. Attendants		
			g. Radio		
		3. Potable Water			
			a. Locations		
			b. Costs		
			c. Health Department		
			d. Radio		
		4. On Course			
			a. Trash Receptacles		
				1. Numbers	
				2. Locations	
				3.Recycling	
			b. Trash Bags		
			c. Carts		
			d. Radios		
			e. Cell Phones		
			f. Credentials		
			g. Schedule		
			h. Responsibilities		
		5. Corporate			
			a. Trash Receptacles		
				1. Numbers	
				2. Locations	
			b. Trash Bags		
			c. Carts		
			d. Radios		
			e. Cell Phones		
			f. Credentials		
			g. Schedule		
			h. Responsibilities		
		6. Dumpsters			
			a. Locations		
			b. Size		

			c. Enclosure	
			d. Letters	
			e. Routes	
			f. Schedule Pre & Post	
			g. Supervision	
			h. Credentials	
			g. Recycling	
		7. Additional		
			a. Tents	
			b. Catering	
			c. Concessions	
			d. Trailers	
	H. Temporary Roads			
		1. Locations		
		2. Type		
		3. Cost		
		4. Tree Clearing		
		5. Dozer work		
		6. Removal		
		7. Restoration		
	I. Mapping			
		1. Orthorectified Aerial of Course		
		2. Create facilities on map		
		3. Update as changes occur		
		4. Uses		
			a. Corporate Sales	
			b. Security	
			c. Police Posts	
			d. Traffic Routes	
			e. Planning	
			f. Implementation	
2. Vendors				
	A. Experience			
	B. Scope of area			
	C. Union			
	E. Schedules			
	F. Equipment needs			
	G. Cost			
	H. Meetings	1. Fall, February, On Site Spring		

			a. Routes		
			b. Recap of previous		
			c. Changes in site		
3. Building Department/Fire Marshall					
	A. Ally vs. opponent				
	B. Requirements				
	C. Site & plan review				
	D. Occupancy Loads				
	E. ADA Requirements				
	F. Meetings Early				
	G. Parking				
	H. Credentials				
4. Police					
	A. Parking & Traffic				
		1. Posts			
	B. Meals				
	C. Threats				
	D. Cost				
	E. Player Escorts				
	F. Lead with State & Federal Agencies				
	G. Requirements				
		1. Phone			
		2. Trailer			
	H. Housing				
	I. Radio				
	J. Call Phones				
5. Parking & Traffic					
	A. Parking Locations				
		1. Type of surface			
			a. Grass		
			b. Rock		
			c. asphalt		
		2. Cost			
		3. Allocations			
	B. Traffic Routes				

	to Parking Areas				
		1. Traffic Engineer			
			a. Cost		
			b. Required		
	C. Parking Company				
		1. Numbers of Attendants			
		2. Cost			
		3. Supervision			
		4. Credentials			
		5. Radios			
		6. Cell Phones			
	D. Directions & Maps				
6. Signage					
	A. On Site				
		1. Type			
			a. Directional		
			b. Informational		
			c. Material		
		2. Size			
		3. Cost			
		4. Installation			
		5. Theme			
	B. Off Site				
		1. Type			
			a. Directional		
			b. Informational		
			c. Material		
		2. Size			
		3. Cost			
		4. Installation			
		5. Theme			
	C. Variable Message				
7. Corporate Tents					
	A. Placement				
	B. Size				
	C. Deck				
	D. Phone				
		1. Numbers			
	E. Scoring				
	F. Decor				
	G. Cable				
		1. High Speed			
	H. TV				

	I. Power				
		1. Quantity			
	J. HVAC				
		1. Size			
	K. Landscape				
	L. Storage Boxes				
	M. Special				
8. Media Tent					
	A. Placement				
	B. Size				
	C. Deck				
	D. Phone				
		1. Numbers			
	E. Scoring				
		1. Quantity			
	F. Decor				
		1. Flags			
	G. Cable				
		1. High Speed			
	H. TVs				
		1. Numbers			
	I. Power				
	J. HVAC				
		1. Size			
	K. Landscape				
	L. Typing Tables				
		1. Chairs			
	M. Score Boards				
	N. Registration				
	O. Restroom Trailers				
		1. Water			
	P. Public Address System				
	Q. Support Trailers				
		1. TV			
		2. High Speed			
		3. Location			
		4. Power			
		5. Steps			
	R. Radios				
	S. Cell Phones				
9. Media Dining					
	A. Placement				
	B. Size				
	C. Deck				
	D. Phone				

		1. Numbers		
	E. Scoring			
	F. Decor			
	G. Cable			
		1. High Speed		
	H. TVs			
		1. Quantity		
	I. Power			
	J. HVAC			
		1.Size		
	K. Landscape			
	L. Catering			
		1. Trucks		
		2. Water		
		3. Furniture		
10. Interview				
	A. Placement			
	B. Size			
	C. Deck			
	D. Phone			
		1. Numbers		
	E. Scoring			
		1. Quantity		
	F. Decor			
	G. Cable			
	H. TVs			
		1. Numbers		
	I. Power			
	J. HVAC			
		1. Size		
	K. Landscape			
	L. Platforms			
		1. Chairs		
11. Photographers Lounge				
	A. Placement			
	B. Size			
	C. Deck			
	D. Phone			
	E. Decor			
		1. Numbers		
	F. Cable			
		1. High Speed		
	G. TVs			
		1. Quantity		
	H. Power			
	I. HVAC			
		1.Size		

	K. Landscape				
12. Merchandise Tent					
	A. Placement				
	B. Size				
	C. Deck				
	D. Phone				
		1.Numbers			
	E. Decor				
	F. Cable				
		1. High Speed			
	G. TVs				
		1.Quanity			
	H. Power				
	I. HVAC				
		1. Size			
		2. Chiller			
	K. Landscape				
	L. Support Trailers				
		1. TV			
		2.High Speed			
		3. Location			
		4. Power			
		5. Steps			
		6. Storage Trailers			
	M. Loading Docks				
	N. Timeline				
	O. Radios				
	P. Cell Phones				
	Q. Restroom Trailer				
13. Pavilion					
	A. Placement				
	B. Size				
	C. Deck				
	D. Phone				
		1. Numbers			
	E. Scoring				
	F. Decor				
	G. Cable				
		1. High Speed			
	H. TVs				
		1. Quantity			
	I. Power				
	J. HVAC				
		1. Size			

		2. Chiller			
	K. Landscape				
	L. Catering				
		1. Trucks			
		2. Water			
		3.Furniture			
	M. Restroom Trailers				
	N. Cell Phone				
14. Trophy Tent					
	A. Placement				
	B. Size				
	C. Deck				
	D. Phone				
		1. Numbers			
	E. Scoring				
	F. Decor				
	G. Cable				
	H. TVs				
		1. Quantity			
	I. Power				
	J. HVAC				
		1. Size			
		2. Chiller			
	K. Landscape				
	L. Catering				
		1. Trucks			
		2. Water			
		3.Furniture			
	M. Restroom Trailers				
	N. Cell Phone				
15. USGA Hospitality					
	A. Placement				
	B. Size				
	C. Deck				
	D. Phone				
		1. Numbers			
	E. Scoring				
	F. Decor				
	G. Cable				
	H. TVs				
		1. Quantity			
	I. Power				
	J. HVAC				
		1.Size			
		2. Chiller			
		3. Split System			

	K. Landscape				
	L. Catering				
		1. Trucks			
		2. Water			
		3.Furniture			
	M. Restroom Trailers				
	N. Cell Phone				
16. Member Hospitality					
	A. Placement				
	B. Size				
	C. Deck				
	D. Phone				
		1.Numbers			
	E. Scoring				
	F. Decor				
	G. Cable				
		1. High Speed			
	H. TVs				
		1. Quantity			
	I. Power				
	J. HVAC				
		1. Size			
		2. Chiller			
		3. Split System			
	K. Landscape				
	L. Catering				
		1. Trucks			
		2. Water			
		3. Furniture			
	M. Restroom Trailers				
17. NBC Hospitality					
	A. Placement				
	B. Size				
	C. Deck				
	D. Phone				
		1. Numbers			
	E. Scoring				
	F. Decor				
	G. Cable				
		1. High Speed			
	H. TVs				
		1. Quantity			
	I. Power				
	J. HVAC				
		1. Size			

		2. Chiller			
		3. Split System			
	K. Landscape				
	L. Catering				
		1. Trucks			
		2. Water			
		3. Furniture			
	M. Restroom Trailers				
18. Player Hospitality(If not Clubhouse)					
	A. Placement				
	B. Size				
	C. Deck				
	D. Phone				
		1. Numbers			
	E. Scoring				
	F. Decor				
	G. Cable				
		1. High Speed			
	H. TVs				
		1. Quantity			
	I. Power				
	J. HVAC				
		1. Size			
		2. Chiller			
		3. Split System			
	K. Landscape				
	L. Catering				
		1. Trucks			
		2. Water			
		3. Furniture			
	M. Restroom Trailers				
19. Concessions					
	A. Vendor				
	B. Tents				
		1. Locations			
		2. Size			
		3. Potable water			
		4. Hand Wash Stations			
		5. Propane			
		6. Health Department			
		7. Dumpsters			
			a. Recycling		

			b. Compactor		
		8. Fencing			
		9. Windscreen			
		10.Landscape			
		11. Theme			
		12. Fire Marshal			
	C. Compound Space				
		1. Location			
		2. Potable Water			
		3. Type surface			
		4. Fence			
		5. Windscreen			
	D. Credentials				
20. Catering					
	A. Vendor				
	B. Tents				
		1. Locations			
		2. Size			
		3. Potable water			
		4. Hand Wash Stations			
		5. Propane			
		6. Health Department			
		7. Dumpsters			
			a. Recycling		
			b. Compactor		
		8. Fencing			
		9. Windscreen			
		10. Landscape			
		11. Theme			
		12. Phone			
		13. Cable			
			a. High Speed		
		14. Fire Marshall			
	C. Compound Space				
		1. Location			
		2. Potable Water			
		3. Type surface			
		4. Fence			
		5. Windscreen			
	D. Credentials				

21. Décor Company					
	A. Vendor				
	B. Tents				
		1. Locations			
		2. Size			
		3. Potable water			
		4. Hand Wash Stations			
		5. Propane			
		6. Health Department			
		7. Dumpsters			
			a. Recycling		
		8. Fencing			
		9. Windscreen			
		10. Landscape			
		11. Theme			
		12. Phone			
		13. Cable			
			a. High Speed		
	C. Compound Space				
		1. Location			
		2. Potable Water			
		3. Type surface			
		4. Fence			
		5. Windscreen			
	D. Credentials				
22. Bleacher Company					
	A. Vendor				
	B. Location				
	C. Dumpsters				
	D. Fencing				
	E. Windscreen				
	F. Phone				
	G. Cable				
	H. Compound Space				
		1. Location			
		3. Type surface			
		4. Fence			
		5. Windscreen			
	I. Power				
	J. Portopots				
	K. Credentials				

23. Electrical & HVAC					
	A. Vendor				
	B. Location				
	C. Dumpsters				
	D. Fencing				
	E. Windscreen				
	F. Phone				
	G. Cable				
	H. Compound Space				
		1. Location			
		3. Type surface			
		4. Fence			
		5. Windscreen			
	I. Power				
	J. Portopots				
	K. Credentials				
24. Landscaping					
	A. Vendor				
	B. Location				
	C. Dumpsters				
	D. Fencing				
	E. Windscreen				
	F. Phone				
	G. Cable				
	H. Compound Space				
		1. Location			
		3. Type surface			
		4. Fence			
		5. Windscreen			
	I. Power				
	J. Portopots				
	K. Credentials				
25. Rental Equipment					
	A. Containers				
	B. Pickup Trucks				
	C. Golf Carts				
		1. Numbers			
		2. Gas vs. electric			
		3. Delivery			
		4. Fueling			
		5. Allocation			
		6. Signage			
		7. Transportation			

		8. Cost			
	D. Fork Lifts & Bobcats				
	E. Light Towers				
		1. Locations			
		2. Quantities			
		3. Fueling			
		4. Placement			
	F. Traffic Cones & Barricades				
	G. Photo Lockers				
	H. Water Truck				
	I. Street Sweeper				
	J. Box Trucks				
26. Fencing					
	A. Vendor				
	B. Location				
	C. Dumpsters				
	D. Fencing				
	E. Windscreen				
	F. Phone				
	G. Cable				
	H. Compound Space				
		1. Location			
		2. Type surface			
		3. Fence			
		4. Windscreen			
	I. Power				
	J. Portopots				
	K. Credentials				
27. Networks					
	A. Compound Space				
		1. Location			
		2. Type surface			
		3. Fence			
		4. Windscreen			
	B. Phone requirements				
	C. Potable water				
	D. Cable				
	E. Vendor List				
	F. Credentials				
28. Faxes &					

Copiers					
	A. List of needs				
		1. Media			
		2. Power			
	B. Barter				
	C. Backup				
	D. Standby				
	E. Special				
	F. Credentials				
29. Bottled Water					
	A. List of needs				
	B. Barter				
	C. Backup				
	D. Standby				
	E. Special				
		1. Truck on site			
	F. Credentials				
30. Admissions					
	A. Gates				
		1. Scanning			
		2. Tents			
			a. Size		
	B. Security				
		1. Pat downs			
		2. Disallowed Items			
		3. Power			
		4. Phone			
	C. Credentials				
		1. Type of access			
		2. Badge or ticket			
		3. Special			
	D. Tickets				
		1. Number			
		2. Type			
			a. General		
			b. Corporate		
			c. Trophy		
		3. Disclaimer			
		4. Hand Book			
		5. Distribution			
		6. Layout & Printing			
31. Programs					
	A. Vendor				

	B. Freight to site				
	C. Storage on site				
	D. Distribution Committee				
	E. Delivery schedule				
	F. Number				
		1. Pup trucks			
		2. Locations			
32. Televisions					
	A. Vendor				
	B. Freight to site				
	C. Storage on site				
		1. Locations			
	D. Distribution Committee				
	E. Delivery schedule				
		1. Number of trucks			
	F. Number				
		1. Sizes			
		2. Type			
33. Furniture					
	A. Vendor				
	B. Needs				
		1. Office Trailers			
		2. Tents			
			a. Type		
		3. Hospitality			
33. General					
	A. Restoration				
		1. Temporary Roads			
		2. Trees			
		3. Trash & Garbage			
		4. Vendor damage			
		5. Asphalt road damage			
		6. Turf damage			
		7. Cart Paths			
		8. Tennis Courts			
		9. Fence			

		10. Other			
	B. Removal Schedule				
		1. TVs			
		2. Copiers & Faxes			
		3. Bottled Water			
		4. Furniture			
		5. Decor			
		6. Trailers			
		7. Electrical			
		8 Generators			
		9. HVAC			
		10. Landscaping			
		11.Tents			
		12. Portopots			
		13. Dumpsters			
		14. Bleachers			
		15. Temporary Roads			
		16. Operations Office			

Timeline

AUGUST

Sunday	Monday	Tuesday	Wednesday	Thursday	Friday	Saturday
					1	2
3	4	5	6	7	8	9
10	11	12	13	14	15	16
Set up Office (on site)						
17	18	19	20	21	22	23
Set up Office (on site)						
					Create Water List	
24	25	26	27	28	29	30
Create Water List						
		Map Site Facilities (on site)				
31						
Map Site Facilities (on site)						

SEPTEMBER

Sunday	Monday	Tuesday	Wednesday	Thursday	Friday	Saturday
	1	2	3	4	5	6
					Print, Review & Approve Facility Locations	
	Map Site Facilities (on site)					
7	8	9	10	11	12	13
	Print, Review & Approve Facility Locations					
14	15	16	17	18	19	20
Print, Review & Approve Facility Locations		Meet with Building Department (on site)				
21	22	23	24	25	26	27
Meet With Building Department			Write Construction Specifications			
			Write Portopot Specifications			
			Write Phone Specifications			
28	29	30				
Write Construction Specifications		Write Electrical Specifications				
Write Portopot Specifications		Write Water Specifications				
Write Phone Specifications		Write Cable specifications				
		Research Vendors				

OCTOBER

Sunday	Monday	Tuesday	Wednesday	Thursday	Friday	Saturday
			1	2	3	4
		Write Electrical Specifications				
		Write Water Specifications				
		Write Cable specifications				
		Research Vendors				
5	6	7	8	9	10	11
	Write Electrical Specifications					
	Write Water Specifications					
	Write Cable specifications					
	Research Vendors					
12	13	14	15	16	17	18
Write Electrical Specifications				Bleacher & Leaderboard Survey (on site)		
Write Water Specifications				Write Ecology Specifications		
Write Cable Specifications				Write Dumpster Specifications		
	Research Vendors					
				Bid Specifications to Potential Vendors		
19	20	21	22	23	24	25
Bleacher & Leaderboard Survey (on site)						
Bid Specifications to Potential Vendors						
	Research Vendors					
	Temporary Road Installation					
26	27	28	29	30	31	1
	Temporary Road Installation					
	Research Vendors					
Bid Specifications to Potential Vendors						

NOVEMBER

Sunday	Monday	Tuesday	Wednesday	Thursday	Friday	Saturday
		Temporary Road Installation				1
			Research Vendors			
2	3	4	5	6	7	8
		Temporary Road Installation				
Research Vendors			Review Bids with Potential Vendors (on site)			
		Meet with Building Department & Fire Department (on site)				
		Security Locations				
			Cable Major Facility Installation			
				Phone Major Facility Installation		
9	10	11	12	13	14	15
		Temporary Road Installation				
Review Bids with Potential Vendors (on site)			Coin Phone Locations			
Building Department & Fire Department (on site)			Major Facility Installation Update			
		Submit Recommendations for Vendors				
16	17	18	19	20	21	22
		Temporary Road Installation				
		Cable Major Facility Installation				
		Phone Major Facility Installation				
	Submit Recommendations for Vendors					
Coin Phone Locations						
Major Facility Installation Update						
23	24	25	26	27	28	29
Submit Recommendations for Vendors			Award Vendor Contracts			
30						
Award Vendor Contracts		Cable Major Facility Installation				
Temporary Road Installation		Phone Major Facility Installation				

DECEMBER

Sunday	Monday	Tuesday	Wednesday	Thursday	Friday	Saturday
	1	2	3	4	5	6
		Temporary Road Installation				
				Cable Major Facility Installation		
	Phone Major Facility Installation					
			Create/Revise TV List		Research Trash Boxes	
Award Vendor Contracts			Create/Revise Cart List			
			Create/Revise Radio List			
7	8	9	10	11	12	13
Research Trash Boxes		Create/Revise Furniture List				
			Meet with Building Department(on site)		Evacuation Plan	
		Temporary Road Installation				
				Cable Major Facility Installation		
	Phone Major Facility Installation					
14	15	16	17	18	19	20
	Evacuation Plan					
21	22	23	24	25	26	27
		Temporary Road Installation				
	Phone Major Facility Installation					
28	29	30	31			
		Temporary Road Installation				
				Cable Major Facility Installation		
	Phone Major Facility Installation					

JANUARY

Sunday	Monday	Tuesday	Wednesday	Thursday	Friday	Saturday
	Let Contracts					
				Cable Major Facility Installation		
	Phone Major Facility Installation					
4	5		7	8	9	10
		Let Contracts		Cable Major Facility Installation		
	Phone Major Facility Installation					
		Assign Phone Numbers				
11	12	13	14	15	16	17
				Cable Major Facility Installation		
	Phone Major Facility Installation					
18	19	20	21	22	23	24
		Review windscreen				
				Cable Major Facility Installation		
	Phone Major Facility Installation					
		Facilities Installation Update				
25	26	27	28	29	30	31
				Cable Major Facility Installation		
	Phone Major Facility Installation					

FEBRUARY

Sunday	Monday	Tuesday	Wednesday	Thursday	Friday	Saturday
1	2	3	4	5	6	7
			Facility Update			
		Cable Major Facility Installation				
	Building Department Meetings					
8	9	10	11	12	13	14
		Facility Update				
				Cable Major Facility Installation		
15	16	17	18	19	20	21
		Facility Update				
		Cable Major Facility Installation				
22	23	24	25	26	27	28
		Review Rental Equipment				
		Cable Major Facility Installation				
29						
Cable Major Facility Installation						

MARCH

Sunday	Monday	Tuesday	Wednesday	Thursday	Friday	Saturday
	1	2	3	4	5	6
		Potable Water Installation				
		Cable Major Facility Installation				
7	8	9	10	11	12	13
		Potable Water Installation				
		Cable Major Facility Installation				
		Building Department Meetings				
14	15	16	17	18	19	20
		Potable Water Installation				
		Cable Major Facility Installation				
		Tent & Floor Construction				
21	22	23	24	25	26	27
		Potable Water Installation				
		Cable Major Facility Installation				
		Tent & Floor Construction				
28	29	30	31			
		Potable Water Installation				
		Cable Major Facility Installation				
		Tent & Floor Construction				

APRIL

Sunday	Monday	Tuesday	Wednesday	Thursday	Friday	Saturday
				1	2	3
				Potable Water Installation		
				Tent & Floor Construction		
				Décor Installation		
4	5	6	7	8	9	10
		Potable Water Installation				
		Tent & Floor Construction				
		Décor Installation				
11	12	13	14	15	16	17
		Potable Water Installation				
		Tent & Floor Installation				
		Décor Installation				
18	19	20	21	22	23	24
		Potable Water Installation				
		Tent & Floor Installation				
		Décor Installation				
25	26	27	28	29	30	
		Potable Water Installation				
		Tent & Floor Installation				
		Décor Installation				

MAY

Sunday	Monday	Tuesday	Wednesday	Thursday	Friday	Saturday
						1
		Potable Water Installation				
		Tents & Flooring Installation				
		Electrical & HVAC Installation				
		Décor Installation				
2	3	4	5	6	7	8
		Potable Water Installation				
		Tents & Flooring Installation				
		Electrical & HVAC Installation				
		Décor Installation				
9	10	11	12	13	14	15
	Potable Water Installation		Electrical & HVAC Installation		Décor Installation	
	Tents & Flooring Installation		Trailer Installation			
16	17	18	19	20	21	22
	Potable Water Installation		Electrical & HVAC Installation		Décor Installation	
	Tents & Flooring Installation		Trailer Installation			
23	24	25	26	27	28	29
	Potable Water Installation		Electrical & HVAC Installation		Décor Installation	
	Tents & Flooring Installation		Landscaping		Trailer Installation	
30	31					
	Potable Water Installation		Electrical & HVAC Installation		Décor Installation	
	Tents & Flooring Installation		Landscaping		Trailer Installation	

JUNE

Sunday	Monday	Tuesday	Wednesday	Thursday	Friday	Saturday
		1	2	3	4	5
		Potable Water Installation				
		Tent & Floor Construction				
		Electrical & HVAC Installation				
		Landscaping				
		Décor Installation				
		Trailer Installation				
		Copier & Fax Installation				
		Television Installation				
6	7	8	9	10	11	12
		Potable Water Installation				
		Tent & Floor Construction				
		Electrical & HVAC Installation				
		Landscaping				
		Décor Installation				
		Copier & Fax Installation				
		Trailer Installation				
13	14	15	16	17	18	19
20	21	22	23	24	25	26
27	28	29	30			

Vendor Contact Information

Stein Consulting LLC-ADA Consultant
Joan Stein President
240 Sharon Drive
Pittsburgh, Pa 15221
412-736-7161
jstein0731@gmail.com

AGL Contracting Inc. - Temporary Roads
Joe Giaquinto
429 Carlls Path
Deer Park, NY 11729
(631) 242-2760

Aggreko-Electrical and Air Conditioning
Dave Prince
10 S. Ridge Drive
Winslow, ME 04901
(207) 859-1982

Andy Frain Company-Private Security
Dane Vontobel
3 Drummers Lane
Newton, CT 06470
(630) 820-3820

API- Television Installation and Direct TV
Frank Tomaino
3117 Route 10 East
Denville, NJ 07834
(973) 328-3328

Arnold Palmer Group- Leaderboards
Gene Bratcher
9000 Bay Hill Blvd.
Orlando, FL 32819
(407) 251-6490

Barton G- Décor
Scott Daffron
6015 the Twelfth Fairway
Suwanee, Ga. 30024
(770) 418-1488

Classic Tents-Tents and Flooring
Robert Kraak
540 Hawaii Avenue
Torrance, CA 90503
(310) 328-5060

Clarence Davids & Company-
Landscaping
Stephen Borden
22901 South Ridgeland Avenue
Matteson, IL 60443
(708) 720-4100

CompSee- Admissions Scanning
Sally Morgan
2202 S. Babcock St., Ste 204
Melbourne, FL 32901
(800) 628-3888

Country Club Services- Parking and
Shuttle
Management
Joe Hughes
454 Morris Avenue
Springfield, NJ 07081
(973) 376-4352

Creative Communications- Radios
Pat McCarty
3332 E. Broadway Rd
Phoenix, AZ 85040
(602) 722-5984

Franzen Graphics, Inc. /Event Solutions,
LLC-Banners
Craig Franzen
5300 Highway 42 North
Sheboygan, WI 53083
(800) 236-2757

Family Chiropractic- Wellness Team for
Caddie & Volunteer Hospitality
Dr. Jeff Poplarski
217 Merrick Road
Suite 204
Amityville, N.Y.11701
(631) 598-7034

Golf Course Analytics- Mapping
Software
David Mikesh
5808 S, Rapp Street
Suite 225
Littleton, CO 80120
(877) 347-2006

Integrated ID-Credentials
Pat Cosmo
1 Integrated ID Systems, Inc.
1150-E Crews Road
Matthews, N.C. 28105
(800) 729-3722

Levy Catering
Jason Kish
805 Pressley Road Suite 110
Charlotte, NC 28217
jkish@levyrestaurants.com
704-634-9619

Mayco Building Services Inc. - Tent Cleaning
Christopher Alex
385 W Main St
Babylon, NY 11702-3023
(631) 587-0255

ModSpace-Office Trailers
Mike Eggert
21201 Cabot Boulevard
Hayward, CA 94545
(800) 523-7918

Mr. John- Portopots and Restrooms Trailers
Jordan Serenkin
200 Smith Street
PO Box 130
729 Keasbey, NJ 08832
(732) 692-2470

MSG Promotions- Hospitality Marketing
Mimi Griffin
1120 S. Cedar Crest Blvd Suite 200
Allentown, PA 18103
(484) 223-3295

New Jersey Fence and Guardrail-Temporary Fence
Jim Hoffman
32 Main Street
Andover, NJ 07821
(973) 786-5400

Pritchard Industries-On Course Trash Removal
David Mayer
2147 Priest Bridge Dr. #5
Crofton, MD 21114
973-919-0269
david.mayer@pritchardsports.com

Prom-Concessions
Bill Givens
484 Inwood Ave.,
Oakdale, Minnesota 55128
(651) 501-8191

Ridgewells Catering- Catering
Andrew Chalfant
5525 Dorsey Lane
Bethesda, MD 20816
(301) 907-3700

Safari Telecom- Communications
Dave Baron
6 Arrow Road, Suite 202
Ramsey, NJ 07446
(201) 934-7400

Salem Sports-Media Décor
Ric Swiggert
Winston Salem, NC
(800) 858-3790

Salopek Golf Cart and Equipment Company Inc.-Golf Carts
Rick Salopek
8765 State Route 201
Tipp City, Ohio 45371
(937) 845-9301

Soco Petroleum-Fueling
Doug Robinson
The SoCo Group, Inc.
Carlsbad, California
(760) 801-0009

T & B Equipment Company- Bleachers and TV Towers
Danny Ellis
11065 Leadbetter Rd.
Ashland, VA 23005
(800) 451-5054

Tournament Graphics- Signs
Phil Clark
24476 W. River Road
Perrysville, Ohio 43551
(419) 878-6508

Transportation Management Services- Parking and Shuttle Management
Mike Moulton
17810 Meetinghouse Rd, Suite 200
Sandy Spring, MD 20860
(800) 437-7629

Index

BIBLIOGRAPHY

(Jeffrey Edward Poplarski, 2011)pp 176-178
(Joan Stein Consulting LLC, 2011)pp 123,126